Charles Henry Sargant

Ground-Rents and Building Leases

Charles Henry Sargant

Ground-Rents and Building Leases

ISBN/EAN: 9783337186845

Printed in Europe, USA, Canada, Australia, Japan

Cover: Foto ©ninafisch / pixelio.de

More available books at **www.hansebooks.com**

GROUND-RENTS AND BUILDING LEASES.

ROUND-RENTS

AND

BUILDING LEASES.

BY

CHARLES HENRY SARGANT,
OF LINCOLN'S INN, BARRISTER-AT-LAW.

LONDON:
SWAN SONNENSCHEIN AND CO.,
PATERNOSTER SQUARE.
1886.

PREFACE.

The following pages are in no sense a legal treatise. They are merely an attempt to deal with some economical aspects of the most ordinary form of house tenure especially in the neighbourhood of London.

I have found it impossible to avoid a somewhat polemical treatment of a few of the "burning questions" of the day. But any proposals to interfere with so elaborate and complicated a contract as that of the building lease, seem to demand the most thorough and searching examination.

C. H. S.

Lincoln's Inn.

CONTENTS.

	PAGE
THE CREATION OF GROUND-RENTS	9
THE DETERMINATION OF GROUND-RENT	24
ARE GROUND-RENTS A ROBBERY?	39
SHOULD GROUND-RENTS BE RATED?	56
LEASEHOLD ENFRANCHISEMENT	85
GROUND-RENTS, ON RE-LETTING, AND CHIEF RENTS	117
THE DETERMINATION OF RACK-RENT AND MONOPOLY	131
GENERAL REMARKS AND CONCLUSION	145
NOTES	156

GROUND-RENTS AND BUILDING LEASES.

ERRATA.

Page 71, line 7, *omit* "and."
Page 120, line 13, *for* "£1 13s. 4d." *read* "£3 6s. 8d."
Page 131, line 3, *for* "substantial" *read* "substantiated."

tempting offers from land-speculators, land-companies, and others, to purchase his land at prices which would yield him an income many times exceeding the rents he has been receiving from his agricultural tenants. And now, having preferred to forego a large portion of this income, in the expectation of the ultimate profit to be derived from personally superintending

GROUND-RENTS AND BUILDING LEASES.

CHAPTER I.

THE CREATION OF GROUND-RENTS.

As London, or one of our greater provincial towns, gradually spreads its network of houses over a larger and larger area, the owner of land lying for the time being on their outskirts, is placed in a position of considerable perplexity and anxiety. If he has been long in the possession of his estate, he has probably received and rejected numberless tempting offers from land-speculators, land-companies, and others, to purchase his land at prices which would yield him an income many times exceeding the rents he has been receiving from his agricultural tenants. And now, having preferred to forego a large portion of this income, in the expectation of the ultimate profit to be derived from personally superintending the development of his land as a building estate, he finds a good deal of difficulty in deciding how best to realise this profit.

For roads and pavements and sewers and houses do not (as might be supposed from the speeches of some eminent land-reformers) suddenly break out as a sort of rash upon building land, to the unmerited advantage of the wicked landowner.

The capital required to lay out, develop, and cover with houses an ordinary building estate, is probably from ten to twenty times the full value of the land. And, if the owner cannot himself provide a sum so enormously in excess of the value of his land, it stands to reason that those, whom he will have to take into what is practically a partnership for this purpose, will secure for themselves a proportion of the profits, which is always very large, and which is in the vast majority of cases determined simply and solely by the higgle of the market.

Let us suppose, for the sake of simplicity, that the landowner is seised in fee, postponing for the present the consideration of the even more common case of his being the tenant-for-life under a settlement. In such a case, according to a recent authority,* "There are in general four courses open: (1) He may enter into a building agreement with a contractor to erect the houses or buildings for him, and when they are completed grant leases at the house rent; (2) (A) he may let the land direct to the builder on building-leases, reserving a ground-rent, in which case the builder may sub-let and thus create leasehold, or, as they are mis-named, improved ground-rents; or (B), as is more usual, he may make an agreement in the first place for building leases, with the condition that the lease or leases shall be granted when the houses have been either covered in or completed, as the case may be, to his or his architect's satisfaction; (3) he may convey the land in fee to the grantee for building in consideration of a perpetual rent-charge; (4) or, lastly, he may sell part of the land with restrictive covenants as to building, in order to secure uniformity with the houses erected or to be erected on such part of the land as he retains."

* Emden's "Law of Building Leases," p. 1.

For the reason indicated above, we may dismiss for the present from consideration the first of these alternatives, though the case is one which theoretically and for the purposes of comparison may be found useful.* The last of the four alternatives is hardly an alternative at all. The part of his land which the landowner sells he does not himself develop. The part which he retains he must develop by one of the three previous alternatives. The third alternative is one extensively adopted in the North of England, and is almost universal in Scotland under the title of feuing. The scheme has great advantages, and will be more fully referred to hereafter; but, as it results in the creation, not of ground-rents properly so called, but only of rent-charges or chief-rents, it need not detain us here.

A fifth alternative, which might have found a place in Mr. Emden's list, consists in the grant of, or agreement to grant, leases at ground-rents, with an option of purchasing the freehold at a fixed rate. This system prevails at Brighton, amongst other places, and was adopted in the

---

* Note (1).

formation of Fitzjohn's Avenue, Hampstead, one of the finest of the recent additions to metropolitan thoroughfares. By this plan, however, so far as the options to purchase are exercised, the landowner parts absolutely with his property; and ground-rents are either not created at all, or are extinguished soon after creation. While so far as the options are not exercised, we have one of the two varieties of the second of the alternatives above stated.

It remains, therefore, to consider for the present the working out, and results, of the second of the above alternatives under either of its two varieties.

Now these two varieties are not, for theoretical purposes, distinguishable from each other. Under either plan, if successfully worked out, the builder will, at the conclusion of his operations (so far as he has not sold to sub-purchasers), find himself the possessor of a number of houses held from the landowner for long terms of years at separate ground-rents. The practical difference between the two plans consists chiefly in the difference of immediate interest given to the builder before he has fulfilled his bargain with the landowner. Under plan

(A) the builder gets an immediate estate in the land, before he has fulfilled his contract; and in case of his failure to fulfil the contract by bankruptcy or otherwise, the only remedy of the landowner would be an action for damages or for re-entry for breach of covenant.

Under plan (B) the builder's right to a lease of any house is dependent on his previous performance of his contract to build that house; and until this contract is performed he has no estate, and no right to an estate, in the land.

As the builder is in general a less substantial person than the landowner, and as the remedy of the latter is practically only personal while that of the former is also against the land, which cannot fail or abscond, plan (B) is far more generally adopted than plan (A).

And it has also this further advantage, that, whereas under plan (A) any purchaser from the builder would be compelled to make inquiries, whether his vendor had fulfilled the obligation to build contained in his lease, under plan (B) the lease is granted only on the completion of the building, contains therefore no covenants to build, and imposes no liability, and therefore no necessity for enquiry, on any subsequent purchaser.

It remains, then, to examine in greater detail the second variety of the second of the four alternatives above mentioned, that, namely, by which the landowner agrees to grant leases to a builder on the completion of houses which the builder is to erect. This, as has already been stated, is the plan most usually adopted, and therefore best understood, in the neighbourhood of London. The bargain is always struck between the landlord and the builder, before any building is begun, and is contained in a rather lengthy and formidable document, commonly called a building agreement. The provisions of this agreement are, in general, to the following effect:—The builder is to enter on the land, and to erect, according to a scheme to be approved by the landowner, a number, varying within certain limits, of houses of a definite character. So soon as the several houses are finished, the landowner is to grant, and the builder is to accept, separate leases of the houses at rents, which are to amount in the aggregate to a specified sum, but whose individual amounts are left to be settled by arrangement between the landowner and the builder, subject to a proviso that no such rent shall be more than a specified proportion (generally one-sixth) of the rack-rental value of the houses. The leases, when granted, are to be in a form specified in a schedule to the building agreement, and always containing a covenant by the lessor to pay all rates, taxes, and other assessment and "impositions." The total rental provided for by the agreement is not to become payable, until a date some two, three, four, or even five years from the date of the agreement; and during the interval a smaller, but gradually increasing rent, has to be paid. If the roads and sewers are constructed by the landowner, the builder has to pay, on taking up his leases, a specified sum for every foot of frontage on a road, by way of payment for such road and the sewer under it. If, on the other hand, the roads and sewers are to be constructed by the builder, special clauses provide for such construction, and also for maintenance, until taken over by the local authority.

There are, of course, numerous clauses in every building agreement directed to secure the due definition, and proper performance of the obligations undertaken by the builder. It often happens, too, in the practical development of a large estate, that a building agreement with respect to the whole estate is undertaken by a surveyor or capitalist, who never intends to build at all himself; but who lays out the estate, and forms the roads and sewers, and then recoups himself by making sub-agreements with actual builders for the erection of houses, which are to be leased from the middleman at a higher rent than that which he has to pay the landowner, and for the same term (less one day) as that which is to be granted to the middleman. And so considerable in practice are the outlay and risk of this middleman, that in London, at any rate, the current rule of thumb is, that the margin of profit of the middleman only begins when he obtains a rent from the actual builders, at least double that which he has contracted to pay to the landowner.

To illustrate this case by a concrete instance:—A landowner agrees to grant leases to a middleman of a building-estate of 20 acres, at a rent of £25 an acre, or £500 in all. Five

B

houses per acre, or one hundred houses in all, are to be built on the estate. The middleman after making roads, forming sewers, and developing the estate generally, is enabled to let off the estate in small portions at a rent which, after allowing for the portion of the land occupied by roads, amounts to £60 per acre.

At the conclusion of the building operations, and assuming that the rents are evenly distributed over the 100 houses, the middleman is in a position to take up leases of 100 houses at £5 per house, and to grant leases of the same houses at £12 per house. The difference of £7 per house is generally known as an "improved leasehold ground-rent"; and it is to the sale of these improved leasehold ground-rents (each of which would, in the case supposed, be worth from £120 to £140) that the middleman looks to recoup himself for his outlay and risk.

These leasehold ground-rents are sometimes sold by the middleman to an outside purchaser, in which case there are already three interests existing in each house, independently of the interest of any occupier. Or, it often happens that the sale is effected, either to the actual builder, or back again to the landowner. In the former of these cases the landowner, by the direction of the middleman, grants leases of the houses to the actual builders at £5 per house, and the builders pay a stipulated price to the middleman for the privilege of obtaining their leases at a rent £7 per house less than they had bargained for. In the latter case the landowner, still by the direction of the middleman, grants leases to the actual builders at £12 per house, and the landowner pays a stipulated price to the middleman for having been provided with a ground-rent £7 per house higher than he had bargained for; or, if the rack-rentals of the houses are likely to be very considerable, the ground-rent may sometimes be still further added to, and fixed at £15 per house. In this case the landowner makes two payments—the first to the middleman, as before, for the raising of the rent from £5 to £12; the second to the builder, for submitting to take his houses at rents of £15, instead of £12, per house. But in every case the lease, as granted, contains no record of all these intermediate transactions, but is, on the face of it, merely a demise at a ground-rent.

It will be seen, therefore, that on a large

building estate, smoothly as the whole thing works out in experienced hands, there are present a multiplicity and complexity of interests calculated to baffle any but an expert in these matters. But, for theoretical purposes, all intermediate interests may be eliminated, and the matter may be reduced to one definite bargain between the landowner and the builder, under which the latter is to build at the rent to be obtained by the former. The work done by middlemen is, in fact, part of the work of the builder, and the improved leasehold ground-rents obtained by them, or the payments made to them by the builder or the landowner, as the case may be, are the return for the builder's work, which they have performed.

It should be noted, however, that the landowner is the only person who obtains a freehold ground-rent, and who will become entitled to the buildings at the expiration of the leases. Any improved rents obtained by middlemen only last during the continuance of the original lease from the landowner. Their interests, and every successive interest, are of a terminable character.

The interest of the landowner is the only

interest called a ground-rent *simpliciter*, and this seems in accordance with theory. For the rent paid to the landowner, so far as it has not been increased under any of the arrangements mentioned above, is the only rent paid for the ground alone. Any improved rent (and also of course any extra rent purchased by the landowner as above mentioned), is rent for improvements effected in the ground.

The rent paid to the landowner does no doubt include a rent for improvements, not only when the landowner has purchased this extra rent, but when he has himself laid out the roads, and generally developed the estate. But in all these cases, inasmuch as the landowner has a freehold interest in the whole rent, including of course a reversion to the buildings, the whole rent is called a ground-rent simply. It is important, however, for theoretical purposes to remember, that large portions of existing freehold ground-rents represent, not rent for the ground, but improvements effected in the ground, which have either been made directly by the landowner, or have been purchased by him from those who have effected them.

Again, it often happens in practice that, as

leases of separate houses are granted to a builder, the total rent to be paid by him is not evenly distributed over the houses. In the instance discussed above, instead of leases being granted of 100 houses at £5 each, there would probably be 40 leases first granted at £10, in order to secure the greater portion of the landowner's rent. The remaining 60 houses would then only be liable to rents of £2 and £1 each, and the middleman would look to this portion of the estate to recoup his outlay, and provide his profit. For here he will obviously be able to secure large improved rents, which he can sell as above stated, either to a purchaser, or to the actual builders, or back again to the landowner.

It follows, therefore, that not only may existing ground-rents be rents for something much more than the ground; but that there may be very different ground-rents on two precisely similar houses, the sites of which were really let on identical terms, and these facts are serious obstacles in the way of any legislation, which should attempt to apply special provisions to that part of the rent of houses which is in fact the rent of the ground on which they stand.

For, with regard to existing houses at any rate, it would be impossible to discover what part of the nominal ground-rent really represented rent for the ground.

CHAPTER II.

THE DETERMINATION OF GROUND-RENT.

It is not intended in the present chapter to plunge deep into political economy, or to discuss the general theory of rent; but merely to consider the causes which, under present conditions, practically determine the amount of ground-rent that an owner of land on the outskirts of a growing town is able to obtain from a builder. It is assumed throughout that there is no monopoly on either side; that the landowner, though naturally anxious to get the best rent for his land, is willing to let it for building purposes, and is not inclined to drive intending builders to other neighbourhoods; and that there are several builders, able and willing to commence building operations, upon remunerative terms.

The rent which will under such circumstances be accepted by the landowner will be the highest rent offered by a reasonably substantial builder.

Now, of course, no builder will offer rent above that at which he expects to build at the average profit obtained in his trade. While at the same time every builder will (in the absence of a " ring ") be disposed to offer as high a rent as possible within this limit, in order to outbid his competitors. The rent accepted will therefore, in general, be the rent at which the most enterprising, or the most economical, or the most sanguine of the reasonably substantial builders expects to be able to build with average profit.

How will this rent be determined in practice by the builder?

Now it must be remembered, for it is a fact often lost sight of, that the business of a builder is to *sell*, not to *let* his houses. No doubt it often happens that the builder lets a house to an occupier, but he lets only because he is for the moment unable to sell, and because he must keep down interest on mortgage-money. And so long as the house is unsold, his capital is locked up to the extent to which the value of the house exceeds the mortgage on it. He is therefore perpetually endeavouring to sell the house, either to the tenant, or to some capitalist, who will buy, subject to the tenancy, and as an investment. It is consequently to the selling-value of a house that a builder must look in making his calculations.

On what, then, does the selling-value of a house, held for a long term at a ground-rent, depend?

Now it may here be useful to explain briefly the method of calculation under which the value of property is determined, by a certain number of "years' purchase" of its annual value. For this method, though simple enough when once understood, is often very perplexing to persons unfamiliar with it.

It is clearly possible to define the relation between the capital value of an investment and the income derived from it, either by expressing the income in terms of (that is, with relation to) the capital value, or by expressing the capital value in terms of the income. The former method is obviously the more applicable, when we know the capital value and want to discover the income; the latter when we know the income and want to discover the capital value.

But, as the income of an investment is in general only a small fraction of its capital value, and small fractions are awkward to handle, we usually multiply the fraction representing income by 100 when we wish to express the income of an investment in terms of its capital value. Or, in other words, we usually consider how many units of income are annually earned by one hundred units of capital, and we express the result by saying that the investment yields an income of so much *per cent*. This is the method habitually adopted when we wish to lend a fixed sum on mortgage, or when we wish to buy an investment the capital value of which is apparent, we inquire how much *per cent.* we shall get for our money.

When, on the other hand, we come to express capital value in terms of income, there is no need to use any multiplier, as the capital value is in general many times the income; and we therefore consider how many units of capital would earn one unit of income. This method is usually adopted when we deal with houses, land, or any other property of which the income is more apparent than the capital value. And we say that such an investment is worth a certain number of years' purchase when we think it worth a price equal to that number of times the income.

Since, then, the rate per cent. earned by an investment may be defined as $\frac{\text{income} \times 100}{\text{capital value}}$, and the number of years' purchase which the same investment is worth may be defined as $\frac{\text{capital value}}{\text{income}}$, it follows that the income of an investment multiplied by the number of years' purchase is always equal to 100.

It also follows that, while the percentage of an investment diminishes in proportion to its safety, the number of years' purchase which that investment is worth increases in precisely the same ratio.

To take two examples. Agricultural land, which till lately was looked upon as the safest of all investments, yielded a very low rate of interest—about $2\frac{1}{2}$ per cent. on the price. The same fact was otherwise stated by remarking that agricultural land was worth forty years' purchase. Again, the goodwill of a profession in which personal qualifications are important —the profession, for instance, of a surgeon or solicitor—is worth a very small number of years' purchase—say about three. The same fact would be expressed by stating that a purchaser of a goodwill of this kind would expect to make $33\frac{1}{3}$ per cent. on his purchase-money.

To return from this digression, which has, however, it is hoped, left no room for doubt in the mind of the reader, the price to be obtained by a builder for his house will obviously be the product of two factors. First, there will be the beneficial annual value of the property; that is the difference between the rack-rent of the property received by the builder and the ground-rent to be paid by the builder. And, secondly, there will be the number of years' purchase which this beneficial annual value is worth.

This second factor varies very largely, even in cases where there is the same length of term to run. Only eight or nine years' purchase is sometimes given for small weekly property where the landlord has to pay rates and taxes, do repairs, and pay a high commission for collection; while for high-class property let on seven, fourteen, or twenty-one years' lease to substantial tenants, who pay all rates and taxes, and keep the houses in repair, sixteen years' purchase, and even a little more, may be given by an investor.

Let it be supposed that in the case in question the class of house which it will pay best to build, and which will be required by the landowner to be built on his property, is of the latter description—that is, suppose it to be a class of house of from £100 to £200 a year clear rental value when let on repairing lease.

The mental process then gone through by the builder is something of this kind. He fixes upon a house of a rental value most suitable to the neighbourhood, as ascertained by his previous local knowledge, or by any information he is able to collect for the purpose. Say, for example, that this house is one which already lets in the neighbourhood at £150 a year, but which will, as he calculates, let only at £140 a year, when he has made an addition to the supply.

He then calculates what it will cost him on the average to build and sell such a house, including in this cost any expenses for making roads and sewers, interest on mortgages, loss of income from capital during construction, and until the house is sold, fees to surveyors, solicitors and others, remuneration for personal trouble, ordinary trade profit, and a margin for contingencies. As a result of this calculation, he finds that he will cover his cost, if he can sell his houses with average rapidity at £2000 each. Now at sixteen years' purchase (which we have assumed is the value of the houses in question) £2000 represents a house of a beneficial annual value of exactly £125 a year. But, *ex hypothesi*, the houses in question can be let at a rack-rental of £140 a year. The builder will, therefore, be able to offer the landowner a ground-rent of £15 for each plot of land sufficient for a house of the description in question.

Such are the considerations, which, directly or indirectly, determine the amount of ground-rent which a builder will offer to a landowner. It is very possible that, in individual cases, a builder does not go through so elaborate a process of calculation as that sketched out above. He may very possibly have heard that another builder has offered a certain rate of ground-rent for land in the same neighbourhood, and has made a profitable speculation, or he may himself have been building in the same neighbourhood, or in a neighbourhood of something the same character, and may thus have formed a fairly good estimate of the value of the land for which he tenders. But these are merely methods by which the builder may make a short cut to an estimate, the correctness of which will still depend on the considerations pointed out above. A proposition in the third book of Euclid assumes conclusions proved by propositions in the first book, without re-stating the line of argument by which those conclusions were reached. But none the less is the correctness of the later proposition dependent on the truth of the reasoning which established the earlier conclusions. And, in like manner, a builder who offers for a building estate a ground rental equal to that which has been successfully paid by a previous builder for a similar estate, is merely appropriating the results of previous experience, and taking a short cut to a conclusion, which is still dependent for its correctness on the line of reasoning pointed out above.

This being so, it appears that any cause which tends to increase or diminish the rack-rental value of property in a neighbourhood falls on the owner of building land in the neighbourhood, to the full extent of the prospective increase or diminution of the rack-rents of the houses which might be erected on his land.* For suppose that in the instance already chosen, through some such cause as the construction of a railway in the immediate neighbourhood, the builder should expect, before entering into his contract, to get a rack-rent of £150 instead of £140 for his houses. The houses would cost no more. The builder would still be sufficiently remunerated by a prospective average price of £2000 per house; and this he would as before obtain, if the beneficial annual value of each house were, as before, £125. But he can now obtain this beneficial annual value, while paying the landowner £25 per house instead of £15. And the landowner can thus appropriate the entire gain on the prospective increase in the rack-rents of the houses to be built on his land.

In the same way, should the neighbourhood in question deteriorate (as many neighbourhoods near London have done of late years), the entire loss will fall on the owner of land yet unbuilt on. The builder calculates that the house he intends to build will only let for £130 instead of £140. But in order to build

---

* See Note (2).

at a profit he would still have to obtain £2000 for each house, which he can only do by obtaining a beneficial annual value of £125; and to obtain this annual value he can only afford to offer £5 annual ground-rent.

Of course, when a contract has actually been signed, it will be the builder who will gain by any rise in the annual value of house property in his neighbourhood between the date of the contract and the time when he has sold to purchasers. The landowner's gain will merely be a somewhat better security for the payment of his ground-rents, and will be of very trifling value. And, on the other hand, any depreciation in rentals after the date of the contract will also fall mainly on the shoulders of the builder. The landlord will still be entitled to, and will obtain, the same ground-rent for the land, and his loss will be limited to losing some part of the security for that rent; unless, indeed, as sometimes happens, the fall in rents, and therefore in prices, ruins the builder before the completion of his contract, and forces the landlord to relet his land, at lowered rents, to a fresh speculator. There are many neighbourhoods in London where a builder, with the additional light of recent experience to guide him, might have offered twice the amount of ground-rent actually accepted by the landlord, and might yet have made a good bargain. There are other districts, again, where builders, with the like additional experience, would not have offered half the ground-rent actually paid; nay, might have refused to build if the land had been offered them rent free.

But these are merely exceptions and variations introduced by the ordinary fluctuations of price common to all businesses. And the broad general rule may nevertheless be laid down, that any increase or diminution in the prospective rack-rental value of an estate, when covered with houses, involves an equal increase or diminution in the ground-rent which will be obtainable by the owner of that estate.*

The point, therefore, of vital importance to the landowner is the amount of rack-rent which the prospective tenant will be likely to pay. For the landowner will gain by the whole of any increase in this rack-rent, and will lose by the whole of any diminution in it.

---

* See Note (2).

To complete the account, therefore, of the determination of ground-rent, the circumstances which determine the rack-rent which a tenant may be expected to pay, must be taken into account.

These circumstances are very various, and must have suggested themselves to every one who has ever had to select a house for himself. Among them are the accessibility of the neighbourhood, the character of the neighbours, the healthfulness of the locality, the presence or absence of good shops, and the amount of the rates. There are many other qualifications, appealing specially either to individuals, or to particular sections of the community. But those enumerated, taking them in their widest sense, are perhaps the most generally felt. It may be suggested that there has been omitted the first, and most important, question that is asked by a house-hunter, namely, whether rents are high in the neighbourhood. But as this last question is itself ultimately dependent on the other circumstances enumerated above, it would be mere circuity of argument to attribute it as a cause of itself. It is undoubtedly true, that a supposed lowness of rents in a particular neighbourhood has a tendency to attract people to that neighbourhood, and so to cause rents to rise there. But the rents have been supposed to be low because people have compared them with rents in some other quarter, and after a further comparison of the relative advantages of the two places in other respects, have come to the conclusion that the relation between these respective advantages is not fairly expressed by the relation between the respective rents. On the whole, therefore, and as a result of the foregoing inquiry, it may be laid down, that the ground-rent which a landowner will be able to obtain, at any time, will depend directly on (but will be subject to larger proportionate fluctuations than) the then prospective rack-rental value of the houses to be built on his estate; and that the rack-rental value of the estate will depend directly on a multitude of other considerations, which may be briefly summed up in the phrase, "the residential advantages" of the estate when covered with buildings.

The ground-rent of the landlord, until actually fixed, is of the nature of a margin, and that a very small margin, on the prospective rack-rental of the estate when covered. A very slight fluctuation in the latter would involve a very large fluctuation in the former in proportion to its amount.

CHAPTER III.

ARE GROUND-RENTS A ROBBERY?

HAVING thus examined the system, under which what are familiarly termed ground-rents spring into existence, and the principles which determine the amounts of those ground-rents, it may be interesting to inquire, whether there is anything iniquitous or unfair in the ground-rent system.

For in many of the allusions which are made to ground-rents, it appears to be assumed that the system is one under which the ground-landlord is enabled to rob one section or other of the community; that is, to appropriate to himself, without compensation, the fruits of the labour and the expenditure of others. Nor can it be doubted that at first sight there is much to support this view.

Suddenly, and without any labour or expenditure on his part, we see the income of a landlord multiplied to many times its previous amount. In lieu of the small ground-rent, which he and his predecessors in title had been receiving for ninety years and upwards, he now becomes entitled to rack-rents of ten or twenty times its value. And, since it is clear that such an accession of income to one individual must involve a corresponding diminution to another, the conclusion is arrived at, that some one or other has been "robbed" by the ground-landlord.

But strangely enough, though it seems quite clear who is the thief, it is by no means so easy to point out the person who has been robbed. The occupier, if he remains in possession, finds the ground-landlord as easy to deal with as was the owner of the ground-lease. And the owner of the ground-lease himself, if he purchased the lease at all recently, is well aware that he paid a proportionately small price for it.

It is also curious that, while every one envies the landlord, who becomes at length entitled to a property much increased in value by the exertions of a former lessee, no one commiserates a landlord who finds his property partially or entirely removed by the exertions of another lessee. And yet this is habitually the case under a mining-lease, which may for many purposes be considered as the exact converse of a building-lease. At the expiration of a mining-lease of coal, the landlord finds that his lessee has been more or less successful in removing the whole of the coal leased to him; and the rent and royalties of the landlord come to an abrupt conclusion in consequence.

But, it will be said, this was the bargain between the parties. The landlord leased the coal to his lessee, knowing that the coal would be removed, and that the property would be delivered up in a deteriorated condition. The rent and royalties paid by the lessee were not strictly income to the landlord, but represented also capital; and a prudent landlord would have set aside a proportion of this rent and these royalties as a sinking fund, to replace the capital that was being exhausted. The answer is, to my mind, complete and conclusive. But does not a similar process of reasoning also apply to land let on lease for the purpose of being improved, of which the most familiar examples are ground-rents? May it not be that, in this case, the landowner is perpetually receiving a rent less than the full ground-rent of his land, because he expects ultimately to have a large addition to the capital value of his property? And, does not the lessee under a ground-lease, get recompense for the ultimate loss of his capital, by the fact that, for a very long period of time, he pays less than the true ground-rent value for his land?

It must have struck every thoughtful person that there must be some explanation of this sort for the apparent paradox. Men are not forced to go into the building trade. Builders are not (at least in popular estimation) a class of men who would easily acquiesce in the appropriation of their property. Many builders make large fortunes from very small beginnings; and there is, perhaps, no trade which affords greater opportunities of success to a man of small means and considerable ability. Nor, again, are the investors who purchase ground-leases with a view to sub-letting, a class of people who would be content to be ultimately mulcted of their capital without some equivalent. We may be sure, therefore, that if the income to be derived from an investment in ground-leases is ultimately to cease, that income will, during the period it has to run, be proportionately higher; or, in other words, that the terminable income derived from a house held on a building lease will (other things being equal) fetch a smaller number of years' purchase in the market, than an equal income from the same class of property which is not terminable.

What the exact theoretical value of a terminable, as contrasted with a non-terminable income is, may be learned from any ordinary actuarial tables. In the best known of these tables, namely, Inwood's, the exact figures for 99 years are not given, while those for 100 years and 95 years are. Taking the rate of interest at 4 per cent. while a non-terminable income is worth of course 25 years' purchase, an income for 100 years is worth 24·505 years' purchase, and an income for 95 years, 24·398 years' purchase. At 5 per cent. a non-terminable income is worth 20 years' purchase, a 100 years' income 19·848, and a 95 years' income 19·806 years' purchase. While at 6 and 7 per cent. the respective sets of figures are 16 667, 16·618, 16·601, and 14·286, 14·269, and 14·263. The values of a 99 years' lease will be something between those for 100 and 95 years respectively, though more closely approximating to the former figures.

It will therefore be seen that, on strictly mathematical principles, there is very little difference between the capital value of a lease for 99 years at a ground-rent, and the fee-simple ownership of the same property, subject to a rent-charge of equal amount. And, as a matter of fact, there is no difference between the market-values of a lease which has 99 years to run, and of a lease which has 98 years to run. But mankind are not governed purely by mathematical considerations; and, apart from the trouble of setting aside from one's income, and investing every year a sinking fund to replace capital, a terminable investment does not appeal to the imagination in the same way as an entirely permanent one. And so, although the capital value of long leasehold house property rarely exceeds 16 years' purchase (at any rate to an investor), that of an equally good class of freehold property would certainly range one year and perhaps two years higher.

If these statements are correct, it follows that the investor in long leasehold houses, so far from being robbed, does as a matter of fact get a better return for his money (after allowing for the formation of a fund to replace capital) than that obtained by the investor in freehold houses. This extra return he is, of course, entitled to retain, as a reward for his superior intelligence in investment, and for his confidence that he will not be led away into treating income as capital in consequence of the terminable nature of his investment. There can be no possible objection to this extra return and no reason for mulcting the investor of it. But I cannot help drawing attention to the singular fact, that the person who has often been supposed to have been robbed, should in fact turn out to have been making a remarkably good bargain all the time.

The above remarks apply to the person who buys for occupation, quite as much as to the investor. In both cases the purchaser buys cheaper on account of the terminable nature of the property purchased, and in each case the saving in price is more than sufficient to compensate for the ultimate loss of capital.

It has been seen, therefore, that a first purchaser of a long-leasehold house and his successors in title (whether such successors be purchasers or legatees) will *together* receive, on an average, an income which will be a full return for the price originally given for the house. But though this is the case on the whole, it is nevertheless interesting to watch how the ultimate prospective loss of income is adjusted between successive owners of the house, when the succession takes place by sale and purchase.

It is said, sometimes, that during the first 30 or 40 years of a London building-lease the capital value of the lease remains unaffected; and that it is only when the number of years of the term yet unexpired are reduced to 60 or less, that a noticeable fall in value takes place. But though this fact may apparently be warranted by experience, it is probably due in great measure to the circumstance that, until recently, the rack-rental value of London property has had a tendency to increase, especially when the character of a neighbourhood has become established. And it is probably true, that there is a slight decline in the value of such long leasehold property (perhaps amounting to one year's purchase) by the time when there are only 60 years of the term left to run. There is said also to be a considerable fall in value between the dates when 60 years and 59 years are respectively unexpired, the reason assigned being that trustees are ordinarily empowered to lend on leaseholds having not less than 60 years unexpired.

After 60 years, or less, are left to run, the value of a lease begins to decline more rapidly. The diminution in price does about coincide with the diminution of the present value of an annuity for a diminishing term of years, calculated at a rate of interest corresponding with that expected to be earned by the class of house in question. But the capital value of the house is always rather less than the actuarial value of the annuity, and is specially less as the unexpired term gets very short. Nor is this due to the existence of covenants in the lease, which may be enforced on its expiration by the ground-landlord. For the last holder of a long lease can almost always manage to evade the performance of these covenants by a simple legal device, known as assignment to a man of straw. And it is indeed an axiom with investors in leases, that the shorter the term of the lease, the higher the rate of interest that may be expected to be realised (of course after allowing for the replacement of capital).

From the preceding remarks it appears that the holders of ground-leases, at whatever time they purchased, are not a class to be pitied. And the same reasoning will show that persons having interests derived out of those of the ground-lessees are equally well protected.

Is it then the occupier who suffers?

If the occupier happens also to be the ground lessee, his case has been already considered. If he is not the ground-lessee, he probably cannot tell you whether the house is held on a ground-lease or not. It may be a freehold house for anything he knows or cares. He has taken the house for occupation at a rack-rent, and whether the rack-renter is a freeholder or long leaseholder makes no difference to him. The bargain made by the occupier is not, and cannot be, affected by the question whether his house is a freehold or a long leasehold, except that in the latter case he cannot obtain from the ground leaseholder an occupation-lease to last beyond the expiration of the term for which the ground leaseholder himself holds.

It has been shown, then, that, whatever appearances may indicate, there is, in fact, under the system of ground-leases no "robbery" by the owner or owners of the freehold of the owners or occupiers of the ground-leases. Occupiers of long-leaseholds are practically unaffected by the tenure existing between their immediate landlords and any superior landlord.* And owners of long-leaseholds are compensated for the terminable nature of their investment by the extra income they receive during its currency. And it has been indicated that the true reason or "consideration" for the enormous ultimate accession of income to the ground-landlord lies in the fact that, for a long period of years, he and his predecessors in title have been receiving a rent less than the full rent, not indeed of the land and buildings, but of the land alone.

This explanation does in truth appear to be the true explanation of the apparent anomaly. It has already been illustrated to some extent by the converse case of a mining-lease. But it is of such vital importance to a thorough com-

---

* But compare parts of Chap. IX.

prehension of the subject, that it may be well to show in some detail how the thing works out in practice.

Let us recur to the example chosen in the second chapter—the case, that is, of a builder who calculates that he can profitably build a house of the rack-rental value (exclusive of rates, taxes, and repairs) of £140 a year, if he can sell such a house with average rapidity for £2,000.

To realise this price, it was calculated that, in the case of a long-leasehold house (which would be worth some 16 years' purchase), it would be necessary to provide a beneficial annual rental of one-sixteenth of £2,000, or of £125. And it followed that the builder could, therefore, afford to pay the landowner a ground-rent of £15 per annum.

But suppose, now, that the landowner is willing to grant to the builder the freehold of the house, when built, instead of a long-leasehold interest in it.* A freehold house is worth one or two more years' purchase than a long-leasehold.†

---

* See Note (3).   † See Note (4).

Suppose that the difference is only one year's purchase in this case, and that, therefore, 17 years' purchase will be given for the house, if freehold. The builder will then have to provide a beneficial annual rental of one-seventeenth (instead of one-sixteenth) of £2,000, or of £117 12s. 11d. He will therefore be able to offer to the landowner an annual payment for the ground of £22 7s. 1d. instead of £15. And the landowner, letting his land on long lease instead of granting the freehold, will thus suffer an annual loss during the continuance of the lease of £7, or about one-third of the income he would otherwise have received.

It appears, then, that under the system of ground-leases the owner, for the time being, of the land foregoes a considerable portion of the income he might otherwise receive, in anticipation of the fact that his successors in title will ultimately receive an extremely large accession of income. And the "robbery" of the system appears to exist, not as between the landowner and the ground-leaseholder, but as between successive owners of the land. A portion of the income of the landowner is continuously and automatically capitalised, until at last the accumulations are handed over to a remote successor in title. The tendency, therefore, of the ground-lease system is distinctly towards the accumulation and concentration of wealth. When the landowner granting the ground-leases is a fee-simple owner on a comparatively small scale, and voluntarily makes such an arrangement, it might be contrary to the usual principles of English legislation to interfere with the bargain. But when enormous quantities of building land are subject to strict settlements, which forbid a building lease for more than ninety-nine years, and when by the peculiar process of re-settlement, common in large landed estates, the whole of a vast and rapidly-increasing property is kept artificially together in the hands of a single family,* we have in operation a machinery for almost illimitable accumulation and concentration of wealth, hardly inferior to that which was contrived in the celebrated Thellusson case, and which has been rendered illegal by special legislation.

It is this marked tendency to the accumula-

---

* See Note (5).

tion of wealth in a few hands which seems to me the most objectionable feature of the system of ground-leases as combined with the system of settlement of land. And it is on this ground rather than on any supposed " robbery " of the ground-leaseholder, that any legislative interference with the system of ground-leases or with the combination of the two systems might best be justified.

A few words may here be said about a complaint made by tradesmen, that in some cases on the expiration of their leases their rents have been unduly raised, on the strength of the goodwill and business connection which they have formed. In a few cases the hardship is said to have been aggravated by the fact that there had been some verbal understanding that this should not be done. But with this latter element of hardship we need not concern ourselves at present. For a distinction must necessarily be drawn by any system of law between enforceable and non-enforceable contracts. And if one man chooses in important matters to rely on the good faith of another, and on the supposition that a verbal " understanding " was really understood, we cannot be surprised if he is sometimes disappointed. We may, and do, pity him who has suffered from any breach of faith, and condemn him who has committed it. But we recognise that there has been at least carelessness on the part of the sufferer, and that such carelessness cannot be provided against by law.

The main complaint, then, of the tradesmen is (to state it as definitely as possible) that, on the expiration of a lease, a landlord sometimes raises the rent above the rent of similar surrounding property, knowing that the expense of moving, and the inevitable loss of goodwill, will compel the tradesman to submit to the extra charge. In fact, the landlord levies black-mail on the goodwill acquired by the exertions of the tenant.

Now, in the first place, it must be remarked, that this hardship is not peculiar to the ground-lease system, but may exist wherever the interest in a shop is divided between owner and occupier. In fact, in many of the cases quoted, the tradesman had only a twenty-one years' occupation-lease. And, therefore, the abolition of ground-leases would not necessarily remove the hardship.

Again, it is, I believe, the fact that on the larger estates in London, which are covered by shop property, it is the rule not to charge for goodwill, but to renew the lease of a shop to which special goodwill value has been added, on the same terms as are granted with regard to similar surrounding property.

Once more, the possibilities of exaction are hardly as great as many persons imagine. Landlords are as unwilling to lose good tenants as tenants are to move. Any attempt to levy black-mail may probably drive the tenant away. And though the tenant on removal may lose a portion of his goodwill, that portion will not in all probability remain with the shop when he is gone. So that the landlord may have both to find a new tenant, and to let the shop, after all, merely at the rent of similar surrounding property.

And, finally, there is no consideration which the reformer must bear more constantly in mind than this, that there are many practices which deserve the severest moral condemnation, and which yet cannot be effectually prohibited by law.

CHAPTER IV.

SHOULD GROUND-RENTS BE RATED?

THIS is a question which has lately been brought into considerable prominence under the rather inappropriate title of the " Taxation of Ground-rents," and which has been referred, with other matters, to a Select Committee of the House of Commons. Their report, when it appears, will, of course, be a most authoritative document, and will probably contain the evidence of the greatest experts of the day. But, in the meantime, it may be worth while to devote some attention to a subject which appears to be very generally misunderstood.

In the first place, it is the rating rather than the taxation of ground-rents, that is sought to be enforced. The proposal is, that the owner of a ground-rent should pay a *pro rata* proportion of the burdens falling on the occupier of the house subject to the ground-rent. Now, with the exception of inhabited house duty, the whole of these burdens are rates not taxes; for income-tax falls not on the occupier but the owner, and is always deducted, under existing circumstances, from a ground-rent in proportion to its amount.

But the question whether ground-rents should be rated divides itself, on further examination, into at least two questions. First, should existing ground-rents be rated? Secondly, should future ground-rents be rated? For the sake of clearness, I will deal at first solely with the first of these two questions (which is, by the way, apparently the more burning of the two), reserving the second question to be dealt with subsequently.

Should, then, existing ground-rents be rated so as to bear a proportionate amount of the local burdens on houses? I have come to a very definite conclusion that this question should be answered in the negative, and for the following reasons, each of which shall be subsequently examined in detail.

First, a definite and well-understood bargain has been made between the owners of existing ground-rents and the owners of the long leaseholds subject to these ground-rents, under which the owners of the ground-rents are to be exempted from the payment of rates.

Secondly, the ground-rent is obtained by the landowner after an estimate has been made, by the builder, of the rates that will have to be paid in respect of the rack-rent of the house to be built. Not merely a proportionate part therefore, but the whole of the prospective annual amount of these rates, has been deducted in fixing the ground-rent. So that the ground-rent in fact already pays the whole rates.

Thirdly, the expenditure of the rates is controlled by the occupiers of houses, and is directly beneficial to them, and to those persons having comparatively immediate interests in the houses; but is only remotely, and to a small extent, beneficial to the owners of the ground-rents.

And, lastly, the effect of compelling owners of ground-rents to pay rates would not, as a rule, be beneficial to the occupiers of houses (that is, to the class whom it is desired to relieve), but would in most cases result merely in a transfer of capital-value from one capitalist to another, contrary to the terms of their bargain.

These four assertions constitute a formidable, and, if substantiated, a fatal indictment of the proposal now under examination. It will be well to examine them separately and carefully.

First, then, as to the bargain between the parties. It will be apparent, from the discussion in the first two chapters, that, except under conditions of monopoly (which will be briefly touched on later), there is the most perfect freedom of contract between landowner and builder. Each landowner is, no doubt, in negotiation with several builders, and naturally endeavours to secure the best terms he can for his land consistently with safety. But, on the other hand, there are other landowners in the field, each desirous of securing an enterprising, respectable, and solvent builder. And every builder, on his part, is most probably in negotiation with several landowners, or has at least managed to gain a shrewd suspicion of their demands.

The rule is, never to commence building operations unless a definite agreement has been previously entered into, and thus neither party can use the position of the other as a means by which to drive a hard bargain. The building agreement itself is an elaborate document, almost always settled by solicitors, and often by counsel, on each side. The form of lease to be granted as the houses are built, is (as stated before) scheduled to, or carefully marked out by, the terms of the agreement. No doubt, in the case of considerable estates, let out in small portions to different builders, the form of building agreement into which the landlord will enter is, for the sake of uniformity, more or less stereotyped. But in drawing up this form the landowner and his advisers have to bear this sobering fact in mind, that, if they insist on unusual or oppressive terms, it is at the risk of losing customers and of having the offers of rent reduced both in number and in amount.

In short, as between landowner and builder, at any rate, the contract is one as carefully considered, as purely voluntary, and as much determined by the "higgle of the market" as can well be conceived.

Of the person who subsequently buys from the builder, either for investment or occupation, it might be sufficient to remark, that he examined the terms of the lease before buying, and takes with full notice of all those terms, including, of course, the invariable covenant to pay all existing and future rates and taxes. But it may also be observed that the interests of a subsequent purchaser are most carefully studied by the builder; for the builder builds in order to sell. If the terms of his leases are unusual or oppressive, he will find great difficulty in obtaining purchasers, and will probably have to take less for his houses. It is, therefore, of prime importance to him to secure usual and beneficial terms in his leases. And, as a matter of fact, ground-leases, at any rate round London, vary very little in their substance, however diversified in expression they may be.

My second assertion was to the effect that ground-rents bear, not merely a part but the whole, of the rates and taxes on the houses on which they are secured. This assertion is probably very startling to many persons, and indeed may almost seem to amount to a paradox.* And yet I believe it to be entirely and literally true.

---

* See Note (6).

In the previous investigation into the determination of ground-rent, it was found that the ground-rent offered by a builder depended upon the rack-rent which it was expected that a tenant would pay for the intended house. And it was also pointed out that the rent that would be paid by a tenant depended upon a great variety of circumstances, including the amount of the rates which he would have to pay. Now no one, who has had any experience in such matters, can doubt that this last point has a very real influence with house-hunters. If there is any reason to suppose that rates are high in the neighbourhood, an intending tenant always makes inquiry on the point; and it is a familiar fact that advertisements recommending neighbourhoods or houses to house-hunters frequently lay stress upon the lowness of the rates, if such is the case. A prudent tenant makes up his mind that he can afford a fixed sum for rent, rates, and taxes; and, if the rates are high, he must *pro tanto* reduce the amount he can afford for rent.

But, if high rates affect the rack-rentals of houses, it follows that they will also affect the ground-rents that will be offered by intending builders of those houses, and that to the full extent of the loss in rack-rental value. For the conclusion arrived at in the second chapter was, that any gain or loss in prospective rack-rentals was thrown, entirely and exclusively, on the ground-rents that could be obtained by a landowner.

And this conclusion is borne out by experience. It is a well-known fact that, in certain suburbs of London, where the rates are extraordinarily heavy, either building enterprise is completely paralysed, or the ground-rents obtainable are exceedingly low. Tenants will hardly offer as much rent as will yield an average return on the value of the buildings alone, because they are so heavily weighted with rates. And an instance, communicated to me by the bursar of one of the largest colleges at Cambridge, is so apposite as to deserve special mention.

It seems that this college owns building land, situate just inside the boundary of the borough of Cambridge, while that immediately outside belongs to other owners. These lands, both inside and out, are, as far as can be judged, of precisely equal natural value for building purposes; but that part of them which is within the borough boundary has the advantage of being a little nearer to the town. It is found, however, that a higher ground-rent can be obtained from builders for that part of the property which is outside the borough boundary, because the rates outside the boundary are lighter than those inside.

This conclusion, that the prospective rates on house property fall exclusively on the ground landlord, which has been here arrived at by an independent chain of reasoning, is, after all, only a particular instance of the general rule of political economy, that all burdens on land fall *ultimately* on the landlord or landowner.

This is a truth recognised by almost every school of political economists, particularly enforced by Mill, and adopted even by so original, or eccentric, a thinker as Henry George. Nor are theorists alone in this opinion. For it is one which is used every day by the greatest statesmen and financiers of our time. When deputations of farmers wait on Liberal ministers with complaints of the depression of agriculture, and with entreaties to be relieved of some of the local burdens on land, they are almost invariably told (and, in my opinion, rightly and properly told) that any relief of this kind would only affect them temporarily, and that the benefit of any relief to local taxation would in a short time be appropriated by their landlords.

I allow that, if, and so far as, after the builder has made his bargain with the landlord, rates are imposed to a greater extent than could prudently have been expected, the loss will fall on the builder, or his successors in title, during the continuance of the lease. But, apart from any such unexpected increase, it does appear undeniable, that ground-rents are diminished by, and therefore bear, the whole amount of rates imposed on the rack-rentals of the houses on which they are charged.

But, it is said that, as a matter of fact, there have of late years been enormous and totally unexpected increases of rates, especially in London; and that under these circumstances, owners or occupiers (it is not quite clear which) of long-leaseholds, should be relieved to some extent of what has turned out a quite unexpectedly hard bargain.

The case should, indeed, be a very hard one, before one of the parties to a contract should be relieved at the expense of the other party from a bargain deliberately entered into; and no sufficient evidence has, as I apprehend, been yet brought forward to justify so startling a proposal.

But, if this increase in rates has been under the direction, and for the benefit of occupiers, or long leaseholders, it is no hardship that ground landlords should not pay for such increase. And if the rating of ground-rents would not really relieve occupiers, it is no use passing a measure which will not remove the hardship complained of.

In fact, the third and fourth of the assertions made some way back have yet to be examined; and this examination shall be proceeded with in the following chapter.

CHAPTER V.

SHOULD GROUND-RENTS BE RATED?—(*continued*).

THE third objection stated in the last chapter to the proposed rating of ground-rents was that the expenditure is controlled by the occupiers of houses, and is beneficial to them and to those persons having comparatively immediate interests in the houses, but is only remotely, and, to a small extent, beneficial to the owners of the ground-rents.

The first half of this objection, that, namely, with regard to the control of the rates, needs little demonstration. It is the occupiers, as such, not the owners, who form the electorate for all municipal purposes. The owner of a ground-rent may have a voice in such election; but, if so, it will be not as owner of the ground-rent, but as occupier of some house other than that on which the ground-rent is charged. It is true that in London the occupiers have only an indirect and imperfect control over very much of their municipal expenditure. But that is only the result of the anomalous and exceptional character of their local institutions, and whatever control is exercised, even in London, belongs to the occupiers, and not to the owners of ground-rents. The occupiers, for instance, elect the vestries, which again elect the greater part of the Metropolitan Board of Works. The occupiers also elect directly the guardians of the poor and the School Board. Owners of property, as such, have no part or lot in determining local expenditure.

If this be so, it would appear to be contrary to ordinary political principle, to make the owners of property directly liable for local expenditure. It is true that *ultimately* (that is, as soon as a fresh bargain comes to be made between owner and occupier) any increased local expenditure will fall on the owner. If, for instance, rates were suddenly doubled in a district, and the average length of unexpired term for which occupiers held their houses in that district were a year and a half, it would only be for a year and a half on the average that the occupiers would bear the extra rates.

For rents would have to be lowered to the extent of the increase in rates (or, at least, to the extent to which such increase was not expended, so as to add to the residential advantages of the district) in order to induce the occupiers to stay, or at least to attract that continuous stream of new occupiers, which must be always flowing into a moderately prosperous neighbourhood, and thus, indirectly, occupiers of land or houses are able to impose burdens on the owners. But still, there is always some check on the disposition to spend at the expense of other people, which might otherwise be aroused in the minds of occupiers. For they will be themselves liable for a year and a half (in the case supposed) to make good the increased expenditure, and at the expiration of that time they will have the trouble and annoyance of negotiating with their landlord for a lowered rental, and, if their negotiations fail, of moving to a fresh house. Such a check as this would not exist could occupiers throw the rates directly and immediately on owners, while any system, which should allow this, would savour of taxation without representation.

That part of my assertion with regard to the

persons who are benefited by local expenditure, will be more fiercely combated. It is, of course, quite obvious that with regard to what may be called ordinary annual local expenditure, it is the occupiers, and the occupiers alone, who are directly benefited. If the roads are kept in good repair, it is the vehicle of the occupier that gains; if the police are numerous and watchful, it is the person and the chattels of the occupier that are protected; if the sewers are well flushed and kept in good repair, the health of the occupiers is improved; if the streets are well lighted, and if parks and open spaces are efficiently preserved and regulated, the occupiers and their families reap the advantage. No doubt the landlord of the occupier is able to charge an extra rent in respect of special advantages enjoyed by his tenant. But as this rent has been previously diminished by reason of the special rates expected to be paid by the tenant, the thing adjusts itself roughly. And the remarks made above with reference to most of the other items of local taxation, also seem to apply to the poor rate (which, however, has not increased of late years), and to the education rate, which is, of course, a comparatively new tax. The ordinary expenditure on these two objects in any one year in a district appears much more directly to affect occupiers in that district than owners; who, be it remembered, are themselves occupiers in other localities, and are rated there roughly with regard to expenditure, and at any rate as measured with reference to the style of house in which they live.

So far, then, as the rates represent ordinary annual expenditure (and by far the larger portion of the rates is of this character), it appears that such expenditure directly and immediately benefits the occupiers in the district rated, and that they are rightly fixed with this expenditure.

But the case is not so obvious, when we consider expenditure outside ordinary annual expenditure. Suppose, for example, that a large capital expenditure is incurred for a purpose, adding to the capital value of the property in the district, such as a main drainage scheme, or the purchase and laying out of a public park. A fresh rate is levied for the purpose (1) of providing the annual interest on this outlay, (2) of providing a sinking fund, whereby the capital expended will be paid off in, say, 50 years. It is in cases of this kind that people feel specially aggrieved, inasmuch as they say that capital value is here added directly to the property of the ground-landlord, while he has not to contribute anything towards the cost of the improvement. Let us inquire, then, in some detail, by whom the extra rate in question ought to be borne, and for the sake of definiteness let us suppose, that the extra rate required amounts to 8d. in the £, of which sum 6d. represents interest on the capital outlay, and 2d. (a high proportion) represents the sinking fund necessary to replace or pay off this capital outlay.

Now it is quite clear from what has been said above, that the 6d. rate ought to be borne by the occupier. He has the use of the main sewer or the park, and derives added health and pleasure from their existence. And he ought clearly to pay interest on the capital outlay, necessary to provide him with these extra comforts, just as much as he should pay the annual expenses of maintaining them in order and repair.

But with regard to the 2d. rate the case is different. The occupier is certainly to the extent of this 2d. rate paying in excess of the extra comfort enjoyed by him, and for the improvements of another man's property. This is unquestionably a hardship, but one of small extent. For the average duration of an occupation tenancy or lease is not long; and at the time of the imposition of any such rate as we are discussing, the occupier will *on the average* have only half of his term yet to run. It will only be for a very few years, therefore, that this payment will have necessarily to be made towards the sinking fund. For at the expiration of the term of tenancy a new bargain will have to be made, and the tendency will then be for any addition to the rates (so far as such addition does not involve a corresponding benefit to occupiers) to fall on the landlord of the occupier, either by causing actual decrease of rent or (perhaps more frequently) by preventing an increase, which might otherwise have been demanded. As between the occupiers of houses and their immediate landlords, then, the payment by the former of such of the rates, as go to form a sinking fund for capital improvements, is a hardship, but a slight and temporary hardship. But the case has yet to be considered as between the owner of the ground-lease of a house (who is himself the landlord of the occupier) and the owner of the ground-rent. I do not enter into any special consideration of the case, where the owner of the ground-lease is himself the occupier, for his interest may obviously be resolved into the two interests of occupier and ground-leaseholder.

To recur to an instance taken before, let us suppose a house of the rack-rental value of £140 per annum, held on a ground-lease at £15 per annum, for a term of 99 years, of which 70 are unexpired. On this house the new 8d. rate in question is imposed, and 6d. of this rate is borne and paid by the occupier, who derives the full benefit thereof. But the remaining 2d. is, *ex hypothesi*, shifted by the occupier, at the conclusion of his tenancy, on to the shoulders of the owner of the ground-lease; and has to be thenceforth borne by him (in the shape of a lowered rental), during the 50 years required to pay off the capital cost of the improvement. It appears to me, that on the above suppositions, the owner of the ground-rent will, at the expiration of the ground-lease, benefit at the expense of the ground-leaseholder to the extent of the capital sum represented by these 50 annual payments of 2d. in the £.

But the hardship to the ground-leaseholder is much mitigated, if not entirely removed, by the fact that he is, in practice, generally enabled to shift not only the 6d., but also the 2d. on to the shoulders of the occupier, who does himself get an equivalent for both sums ; and this for the following reasons. First, permanent improvements undertaken by the local authority are generally much needed, are worth more than they cost, and add more to the annual value of the property affected by them than is represented by the *interest* on their cost. Secondly, even supposing that the capital cost of permanent improvements adds merely an equivalent capital value to houses in the district, the local authority is always able to borrow at a much lower rate of interest, than is obtained by the ground-lessees of houses. And in general, therefore, the annual value added to a house by a capital improvement by the local authority, say of £100 in respect of that house, is sufficient to meet not only interest on this sum, as borrowed by the local authority, but also a small extra annual sum for the purpose of the necessary sinking fund. And, thirdly, it cannot be assumed that the capital improvement effected by such a scheme as is being discussed, will be ultimately beneficial to the ground-landlord, to the full extent, at any rate, of the value of the improvement, when made. Our main drainage system, for instance, may have to be radically and entirely altered, while most public works, after existing for a certain number of years, require renewal (if not entire reconstruction), at a cost far exceeding the ordinary cost of annual repair.

But notwithstanding these considerations, there does seem to me (apart from the question of bargain) a distinct residuum of grievance and hardship to the long-leaseholder. The grievance, however, is in regard to so very insignificant a portion of the rates, the difficulties of apportionment between ground landlord and ground-lessee would be so great, and the bargain between them (made partly to obviate this inconvenience) is so distinct, that the case does not appear to be one for legislative interference.

There has yet to be examined the fourth objection to the rating of ground-rents, viz., that it would not, as a rule, be beneficial to the occupiers of houses, but would in most cases result merely in a transfer of capital value from one capitalist to another, contrary to the terms of their bargain. The proof of this assertion is much facilitated by, and, indeed, is almost involved in, the preceding discussion ; but it may be well to devote some attention to the direct treatment of the question.

In most of the arguments put forward by the opponents of the ground-rent system, it appears to be assumed, that the occupier of the house is in general the owner of the ground-lease ; and that, therefore, the question, whether of rating or of enfranchisement, is one between owner and occupier.

The assumption is a mere delusion. As a matter of fact in London, at any rate, the great majority of occupiers even of highly-rented houses are not the owners of the ground-leases of their houses. There is usually, at least, one interest intervening between that of the ground-landlord and that of the occupier. Sometimes there are two, three, or even more intervening interests. But the typical case may be taken to be one in which there are a ground-landlord, a ground-leaseholder, and an occupier.

The reasons for this separation of interests are not far to seek. No doubt there is some attraction to the occupier in the prospect of acquiring the ground lease. For if he purchases he will, during the remainder of his tenancy, be earning 6 or 7 per cent. on his purchase-money, (after allowing for replacement of capital) without any risk. But, on the other hand, his capital will be, to a certain extent, locked up; and in case he should wish to change his residence, for any one of an infinite variety of reasons, he will be unable to do so without the expenses and risks of realisation. And so the great majority of occupiers prefer to remain occupiers, and to purchase immunity from risk and restraint by paying a rent considerably higher than the interest on the purchase-money of a ground-lease. And, it may be incidentally remarked, this would probably be, at least, as much the case, were the question one of purchasing the freehold of a house instead of the ground-lease. For though, on the one hand, there may be more of the sense of ownership in holding the freehold, than in holding a lease however long; there would, on the other hand, be the disadvantages of obtaining a somewhat lower rate of interest on the purchase-money, and also of acquiring an interest to which, in the present state of the law, at all events, it is rather more difficult and costly to make title, than to a long leasehold interest.

But, whatever the reasons for it, the fact remains. Occupiers of houses are not, as a rule, the owners of the ground-leases. These persons are generally capitalists who have purchased the ground-leases upon the calculations of loss and gain ordinarily affecting investors. And the operation of any law, directing that rates might be deducted *pro rata* from the ground-rent, would probably be as follows:—

During the residue of his occupation term (say some two or three years, on an average), the occupier would still primarily pay all the rates, but would ascertain from the owner of the ground-lease what the amount of the ground-rent was, and would deduct from his rack-rent the rates on that amount of ground-rent. The owner of the ground-lease would make a similar deduction, in his turn, from the ground-rent payable to the ground-landlord.

And, so far, the only gainer would be the occupier, who would be relieved, be it observed, of an amount of rates depending on a bargain between two other persons with which he never had anything to do, of which he was probably quite ignorant down to that time, and which certainly never influenced him in the least when he made his contract of tenancy.

But, on the conclusion of the occupation term, the whole advantage will accrue to the owner of the ground-lease. For there is no reason why the occupier should not be prepared to pay as much, as before the alteration of the law, for rent, rates, and taxes together. But his rates have now been diminished, and to the extent of that diminution will the occupier be able to offer an increased rent.

In the case we have hitherto been discussing of land covered with buildings for the first time, the ground-rent of a house generally bears so small a proportion to its rack-rental, that the gain to the owner of the ground-lease would probably not be so noticeable as the loss to the owner of the ground-rent. But where, as in the City of London, the value of the land bears a very large proportion to the value of the buildings, the injustice of any such legislation is more striking.

In a case that recently came within my knowledge, land in the City was let on ground-lease at a rent of £1,400 per annum, and the lessee covenanted to erect buildings on the land of the value of £10,000 at the least—the annual value of the buildings being therefore about £700 per annum, or half the annual value of the land, or one-third the value of land and buildings. Cases, no doubt, often occur in which the annual value of first-class sites in the City is far more than double that even of the palatial buildings erected on them ; but the case above stated is quite strong enough an example.

In this instance the lessee must have calculated that the rack-rental value of the land and buildings would be at least £2,100 ; that is, that an occupier would pay that for them, do all repairs, and defray rates and taxes. Rates at 5s. in the £, assuming the property to be fully rated, would amount to just £525, for the ordinary one-sixth is not strictly deductable when the tenant repairs. Assume that, before the lessee let the land and buildings, rates were by legislation charged on ground-rents *pro rata*, in spite of agreement to the contrary. Of the £525 rates, £350 would in future have to be paid by the ground landlord, and only £175 by any occupier. The owner of the ground lease could at once raise the rent demanded by him by £350, that is, to £2,450; and he would be in future entitled to a beneficial annual value of £1,050 instead of £700; that is, his income would at one stroke have been increased one-half, at the expense of the ground-landlord, and without any benefit to the occupier. There appear to me, then, for the foregoing reasons, to be insuperable objections to the proposal to rate existing ground-rents.

But we have still to examine the proposal to rate directly ground-rents created in the future, and to prohibit any bargain between ground-landlord and ground-leaseholder, that the latter should pay all the rates. This proposal is not liable to any objection on the ground of confiscation, and it is urged in its favour (1) that the ground-landlord will thus have a practical interest in his property which he does not at present feel; (2) that a feeling of injustice will thus be removed, since the landowner will thus pay rates, apparently as well as actually. To the first of these arguments it may be replied that it would be a mockery to give the ground-landlord a "practical interest" in the rates on his houses, unless you also give him a share in the control over their expenditure; and to the second, that the science of government must have reached a low ebb if an otherwise fair and convenient arrangement must be prohibited by legislation, because its fairness is not apparent on the surface, and is only revealed after a long and technical examination. But the true answer to these arguments really lies in the overwhelming convenience of the present system, as compared with that proposed. It would be an extraordinary system under which one item, and one item only, of the rack-rent of a house should be charged on an owner, and the residue should be paid by the occupier. Indeed, in the case of agricultural land, where we have, as a rule, only the two interests of freeholder and occupier, an agitation is now going on for the adoption of the Scotch system, under which the whole rates are divided equally between landlord and tenant. And there is no special reason why this last proposal should not be next made with regard to houses. But it is obviously a totally different proposal from that of rating ground-rents. Practically, at any rate in towns, the custom of the occupier paying all the rates has been found to work well ; it is not peculiar to places where the ground-lease system prevails, but is as universal where houses are mostly freehold ; and the mere fact that it furnishes an apparent though unreal grievance for agitators, should not of itself be sufficient to cause its prohibition by the Legislature.

CHAPTER VI.

LEASEHOLD ENFRANCHISEMENT.

ANY one who has carefully examined the arguments in the previous chapters of this essay will, I hope, be convinced that the ground-lease system is not open to the charge of robbery, at any rate as between ground landlords and ground leaseholders. But it by no means follows that the system of ground-leases may not be condemned for other reasons. If, for instance, this system encourages "jerry-building," promotes improper house-jobbing, or discourages the proper repair or improvement of house property, it is to this extent a bad system; while if the evils in question attain large proportions, and are not compensated for by corresponding advantages, it may well be that the system should be discountenanced, or even absolutely prohibited, by the Legislature.

Now, all these charges, and many others, have been brought against the system of ground-leases, and, as a means of obviating the evils in question, a proposal has been put forward, and extensively supported, for enabling lessees to compulsorily purchase from their ground landlords the fee simple of their houses. This proposal is put before the public in its most definite shape in a little book on leasehold enfranchisement, written by Messrs. Broadhurst and Reid, and forming one of the Imperial Parliament series.

The earlier chapters of this book treat of the hardships and evils existing under the present law. With the statements in these earlier chapters it is not now proposed to deal at all exhaustively; space forbids any such attempt. But a few general observations may usefully be made on some noticeable features in these chapters.

The most numerous and the most telling of the cases of hardship recorded in the first chapter are cases arising under the Cornish system of leases for lives. Leases of this kind are, no doubt, injurious, as partaking of a speculative, or even gambling, character; and there seems little reason why they should not in future be absolutely prohibited by legislation.

But they are fast dying out, are of comparatively minor importance, and are not treated of in the present essay. It must be remembered, too, that the cases selected by the authors are always those where the speculation proved unlucky for the tenant, not those where the landlord was unfortunate.

Again, the argument in the first and second chapters is much assisted by the *petitio principii* involved in speaking of the house dealt with as the leaseholder's, and then proceeding to make use of the implication contained in the phrase that the house *belongs* to the leaseholder. If the house *does* so belong, it is manifestly unfair, and even iniquitous, that it should be suddenly transferred to the landlord. But there is nothing contrary to any principle of natural justice in an arrangement under which a house, a piece of land, or any other material object should be the property of one man for a definite period and of another at the expiration of the period. A house is often loosely spoken of as the occupier's, though that occupier may have only an annual, a monthly, or even a weekly tenancy. Yet it would be manifestly unfair to adopt this use of popular parlance so as to imply that the house was the property of the occupier.

And, thirdly, the arguments against the system are obviously overstated and unduly multiplied. And it is interesting, as illustrating the spirit in which the work is written, to compare two statements on pages 40 and 71 respectively. On page 40, the system of ground-leases is condemned as "conferring upon landlords a degree of authority, and a right of interference in regard to the homes of the people, which is unendurable in a free country"; on page 71, the authors complain of "the want of control by landowners who have granted long leases."

These quotations are illustrative of the mental flabbiness which oppresses politicians when discussing the rights of "the people." If "the people" are holders of long leases direct from the landowners, the conditions of these leases are "unendurable." But if the long leases have been purchased by investors, and "the people" are tenants of these investors, the pity is that the conditions of these leases are not yet more "unendurable"; and that they are not harshly and oppressively enforced by the landowners, to the ruin perhaps of the investors, but (as is supposed) to the benefit of "the people."

It would be an instructive exercise for Mr. Reid, or any other eminent counsel, to attempt to devise a form of tenancy on behalf of a lessee which should be open to neither of these two objections.*

The remainder of Messrs. Broadhurst and Reid's book is occupied with the suggestion of a remedy for the evils of the ground-lease system. This remedy consists in enabling any lessee, who has twenty years of his lease unexpired, to compulsorily acquire the interest of his immediate landlord, at the price which would, in the opinion of a county-court judge, be accepted by a willing vendor from a willing purchaser. By this method a lessee, though he should not himself be immediately in relation with the ground landlord, would be enabled to acquire successively all intermediate interests, and at last to obtain the ownership of the fee simple. The bill introduced into Parliament for this purpose by Mr. Broadhurst is printed

---

* See Note (7).

in an appendix to the book; and another appendix contains a bill for a similar purpose, which acknowledges the paternity of Lord Randolph Churchill.

Now, deferring for the moment any criticism of the details of Messrs. Broadhurst and Reid's scheme, it may be interesting to deal first with the general character of the evil they propose to remedy, and the nature of the treatment they prescribe. And the first remark, which must occur to any person at all acquainted with the subject, is that both in their diagnosis of the malady, and in their prescription of remedies, the joint authors have almost entirely ignored the most important element in the case.

This element consists in the fact that occupiers, in London at any rate, and especially occupiers of the poorer class, are not, as a rule, the owners of the ground-leases of the houses in which they dwell. Poverty may often be one reason: but that it is not the sole reason is conclusively proved by the fact, that many a wealthy man with realised capital, far exceeding the value of the house he occupies, does not invest in the purchase of the ground-lease of his house, but prefers to pay a rent considerably exceeding the income derived from the investments representing the purchase-money for the ground-lease. And the reason for his hesitation has been, to some extent, indicated in a previous chapter, and is, indeed, sufficiently obvious. Houses are not, and never can be, an easily realisable property. Apart from the legal charges incident either to a purchase or a sale, the expense of employing auctioneers and surveyors is necessarily very high. And even after the property has been extensively and expensively advertised, there is no security that it may not, after all, have to be disposed of at a heavy loss.

Now, there are a thousand-and-one circumstances which may make a man wish to leave his house. His means may increase or decrease, his family may grow or diminish, his business or pleasure may make him wish to change his present neighbourhood. And the consequence is that, from purely natural considerations, which no legislation can abrogate or modify, the great majority of occupiers are not, and do not wish to become, the owners of their houses. They prefer that houses should be provided for them at a rent. And this service is performed for them by capitalists, who incur no particular odium when they buy an expensive class of house, to let to persons of means; but who are liable to be stigmatised as middlemen, if they buy a poor class of house to let to poor occupiers.

Now, the case for leasehold enfranchisement is perpetually put forward by our authors (if not expressly, yet impliedly) on the ground that it will enable occupiers to become the owners of their own houses, and will thus prevent the manifold evils which arise, when one man resides in the house belonging to another. But not even Messrs. Broadhurst and Reid propose that *any occupier* should be enabled to purchase the interest of his immediate and his superior landlords. Such an interference with contract would be too monstrous and palpable. Yet, unless some such step is taken, very little will have been done to attain the desired consummation. For, as the proposal at present stands, the only person who would be enabled to acquire the freehold of a house would, in most cases, be the capitalist who had invested in the purchase of the ground lease. Now, as before remarked, this capitalist is, in the case of the poorer class of houses, nothing but the "middleman." And the first effect of the Leasehold Enfranchisement Scheme would be to hand over the poorer occupiers in London to the tender mercies of that hated "middleman," over whom Messrs. Broadhurst and Reid consider it so necessary for the great landowners to have additional powers of control.

This result is startling, and yet it is unquestionable. To some considerable extent, in the wealthier portions of London, and to a smaller extent in the poorer, respectable neighbourhoods, occupiers would be enabled by the proposed Bill, to become the freeholders of their houses. But, in far the larger number of cases, even in these districts, and almost without an exception in the real slums of London, it would be the intermediate capitalist or middleman, who would acquire the absolute ownership of the property. And, therefore, from the point of view of the housing of the poor, the question seems to reduce itself to this : Is it better that the immediate landlord of the poorer classes should be a middleman who is a freeholder, or a middleman who is a ground-leaseholder?

Now it has always seemed to me a great pity that the immediate landlord of the poorer classes in towns should be so generally held up to public contempt and execration. The poorer classes cannot and will not provide or purchase their own houses; and, as houses have to be provided for them somehow, there must also necessarily be landlords. Now though, in the great majority of cases, the working classes do strive, to the best of their ability, to pay their rents honestly and punctually, yet there are black sheep among them, as among every other class, and a landlord of this sort of property is compelled to exercise a watchfulness, and occasionally a firmness, which may sometimes degenerate into suspicion and harshness. The immediate effect of this is, that investors of the better class will not touch a kind of property which brings them into such unpleasant relations with a class below them. And this disinclination is immensely increased by the popular indignation which is levelled at the owners of tenement houses. So that, in the end, investments of this description are left to the less respectable class of investors, who expect a rate of interest rendered additionally high in consideration of the unpleasantness of their position. The true remedy for many of the evils under which the poorest occupiers suffer, is to be found in the thorough recognition of the fact that the relation of landlord and tenant is a perfectly fair and honourable one on both sides. For it will only be then that dwellings will be provided for, and let to, the poor by an averagely conscientious set of investors. It is, indeed, by the recognition of this fact that both Sir Sydney Waterlow and Miss Octavia Hill have achieved such great practical good.

But, to return from this short digression, the main position that must be established by the advocates of leasehold enfranchisement is, that occupiers will be better housed under a landlord who is a freeholder than under one who is a ground-leaseholder. The subject is a wide and complicated one, and I may frankly confess that I am not able to decide to my own satisfaction which is the better system ; and that I should be disposed to leave the matter to be adjusted by the natural laws of supply and demand, which, however, could not be effected except by some alteration in the present law. But it may be well to point out a few practical considerations on either side of the question.

In the first place, it must not be supposed that the immediate landlord, when a freehold system prevails, will be a very different person from the immediate landlord under a leasehold system. Under the present system the freeholders are often great landowners, who receive only the ground-rents of the houses, are not brought into immediate contact with occupiers, and are therefore often advantageously contrasted with the ground-leaseholders or middlemen, who look to the rack-rents for their income. But these great landowners would certainly not face the trouble and odium of collecting the rack-rentals of houses on their property. And even if they did, they would find it necessary to adopt a very different attitude from that which benevolent enthusiasts wish them to assume at present. So long as they are secure in the possession of the ground-rents merely, it would not affect their income to insist upon the owner of an existing ground-lease putting the house into a state of thorough sanitary repair, in accordance with the strictest interpretation of the covenants in his lease. But directly they come into the enjoyment of the rack-rents, any such expenditure would fall on their own shoulders; and they would not be less amenable to business considerations than other classes of society.

A better example could hardly be furnished than that given on pp. 47 and 48 of Messrs. Broadhurst and Reid's book, with regard to the renewal of the leases on the Northampton estate. As the existing leases fell in, the Marquis became of course the freeholder in possession, and was entitled to the rack-rents. Now we find that in the case of houses which did not require immediate rebuilding, that is in the case where he was in the ordinary position of a freeholder of houses in direct relation with the tenants, he did not collect the rack-rents, but let out the houses again for short periods, on condition of certain repairs being executed. And we also find that in those cases where any increase in the repairs demanded would have necessitated a diminution in the rent offered by the lessee, the Marquis did not insist on certain expensive repairs

G

which were necessary to put the houses into a thorough sanitary state.

A great deal is made of this evidence, as illustrating the defects of the ground-lease system. I maintain, on the contrary, that it illustrates the evils of the freehold or, indeed, of any system of tenure. Here was a great nobleman in the position of the actual freeholder in possession, and yet even in this case we find the freeholder, or his agents, governed by business considerations, and declining to insist upon sanitary improvements which would involve a loss of income. No attempt is here made to judge the conduct of the Marquis of Northampton, who may very probably have been hampered by settlements. What I wish to point out is, that freeholders cannot be trusted more than leaseholders to neglect their pecuniary interest. Mr. Boodle says that the Marquis of Northampton is in future going to collect the rack-rents of his houses, as the leases fall in, through a lady visitor. This is, no doubt, an admirable system when well worked. But it is improbable that any large proportion of rack-rents in the poorer districts of London can be permanently collected on this plan, while that there is an opportunity of trying it at all on a large scale is in fact due to the Northampton property having been previously built over on ground-leases, which are now expiring.

Under any system, therefore, it may be laid down that the immediate landlord of the occupier will be of much the same class, and will be governed by much the same considerations as at present.

But it is further alleged against the ground-lease system, first, that it promotes "jerry-building" to an extent which is not the case under a freehold system; and, secondly, that it results in houses being allowed to fall into a dilapidated, and even ruinous state, during the last few years of the terms granted by ground-leases.

With regard to the first of these objections, it is obviously immaterial to the owner of a ninety-nine years' ground-lease, whether the house leased stands up or falls down at the expiration of the ninety-nine years. And any additional expenditure in the construction of the house, which should affect its durability after the end of the lease, would be money thrown away by the owner of the lease. It is, therefore, unquestionable that to this extent the tendency of the ground-lease system is to produce a less solid kind of house than might otherwise be built. But this tendency is to some extent checked by the restrictions and conditions as to building, imposed by any well-drawn building-agreement. While, again, it is by no means easy for a builder to build that which will last just ninety-nine years and no more. In fact, jerry-building is a style of building which lasts not for ninety-nine years, but for a much shorter period; the real temptation to a builder being to build only just sufficiently well to last until he has sold the property.

"Jerry-building," indeed, exists and flourishes under a freehold as well as under a leasehold system of building. In fact, under the former system the jerry-builder is less hampered than under the latter. For, under a freehold system, there is no ground-landlord who has an interest in the construction of buildings which may last until the term of the lease has expired. And indeed it is notorious that under the leasehold system, where the nature of the property required it, the most palatial and substantial buildings have been constructed; while under the freehold system, where no sufficient extra gain was to be obtained by good workmanship, and there was no adequate public supervision of buildings, the most wretched properties have been "run up." "Jerry-building," therefore, is, in my view, referable to causes altogether independent of the ground-lease system.

For the second charge against the ground-lease system rather more reason exists. No doubt during the last few years of a ground-lease the ground-leaseholder has no sufficient inducement to cause him to substantially repair the property. And during this period a house may be allowed to deteriorate more than would otherwise be the case. But this deterioration has very definite limits; for, however short may be the period of the unexpired term, it is still as necessary as ever to secure rent from occupiers. Every deterioration means, *pro tanto*, a loss of rent, while, if deterioration goes too far, rent will cease altogether; and therefore a ground lessee is always likely to keep the house leased in at least a tenantable condition, since he has always to attract or retain occupiers, who, be it remembered, are not concerned with the state of the bargain between their landlord and any superior landlord.

CHAPTER VII.

LEASEHOLD ENFRANCHISEMENT—(continued).

In the last chapter there were discussed many of the current objections to the building-lease system. There have now to be mentioned some of the practical advantages of the system, which are often overlooked, but which appear to me to be of considerable importance. And in the first place must be mentioned the practical stimulus, which is afforded by the system, to the rebuilding, or the thorough repair and renewal of houses at definite intervals.

It must be remembered that, when a house in London needs to be pulled down and rebuilt, the rent of the land on which it stands, though much higher than at the time when the house was originally built, is yet much lower than the rack-rental of the house. And under a freehold system of house tenure the freeholder, having been accustomed to receive the rack-rents of the house, is naturally unwilling to do anything which will involve a loss of income, until he is absolutely compelled. Under this system, therefore, owners of houses are under a strong and continuing inducement to defer re-building or thorough renovation, till long after the proper period.

Now, under the ground-lease system, a freeholder who has only been hitherto receiving a small ground-rent, suddenly finds himself entitled either to receive the rack-rents of the house, or to re-let the ground at an advanced ground-rent. In his case, therefore, to refuse the larger return and accept the smaller, is to forego part of an addition to income, not to submit to an actual reduction of income. It follows, then, that under the ground-lease system on the falling in of the leases, houses are generally either entirely rebuilt or are renovated and improved to an extent beyond what might be expected under a freehold system.

Another advantage of the building-lease system is the great additional opportunity afforded for the ultimate improvement of town property, when the ground-leases of large blocks of houses fall in nearly simultaneously. For many improvements, which would involve a loss to a small owner, may be profitably undertaken by, and indeed are only possible to, the proprietor of a large and continuous property. The widening of streets, the removal of dilapidated and unsightly buildings, and the development of a large and comprehensive scheme of re-building can never, practically, be carried out where property is minutely subdivided. Indeed the first and most important requisite of such a scheme as the well known Birmingham Improvement Scheme, is to vest the whole of the property in a district in one ownership—in that case the ownership of the Birmingham Corporation.

One further advantage is sometimes claimed for the ground-lease system, namely, that residential advantages are afforded by it to the occupiers on a great estate. To some extent the claim is a just one. But the advantages thus afforded to one class of society seem to be counterbalanced, or, indeed, even outweighed, by the disadvantage resulting to society in general from the consequent separation in locality and interest of its various constituent elements.

It has been shown, then, that the arguments

in favour of converting a long-leasehold system of house tenure into a freehold system are very much weaker than is often supposed, and that there are actually some points in which the long-leasehold system is superior to the freehold. And if the present system had arisen quite spontaneously and under conditions of absolute freedom, there would, in my view, be no sufficient ground for legislative interference with the existing condition of things. I have hitherto put aside, and do not yet mean to consider the effect on rent contracts or building contracts of monopoly in the ownership of land. Monopoly is a peculiar phenomenon, demanding very special treatment, and any legislation which should apply to cases where monopoly has not existed, principles properly applicable only in cases of monopoly would probably be both mischievous and ineffectual. The freedom now alluded to is the freedom possessed by an absolute owner of land to develop its resources, and generally to deal with it in the most beneficial manner.

It has been stated that a fee-simple owner, letting his land for building purposes, can either lease for a term of years at a rent, or can reserve a rent-charge on a grant in fee; and reasons have been given to show that in the latter case his immediate income would probably be larger than in the former.

Now, if this fee-simple owner voluntarily foregoes his immediate income for the sake of the ultimate return, it would be, to say the least of it, a strong proceeding to interfere with the bargain he has made. But a large proportion of the land in this country is not owned in fee simple by any one individual, but is subject to settlement of one kind or another, and many of these settlements are perpetually renewed from generation to generation under a highly artificial process. This settled land can only be leased for any considerable period under special powers inserted in settlements, which powers do not, in the vast majority of instances, authorise the grant of any building lease for a longer period than 99 years. The powers, too, of ecclesiastical corporations, who are also large landowners, are similarly limited, and the consequence has been that builders and investors have been often compelled to accept long leases where they might otherwise have desired freeholds.

This compulsion, though often effective, has never been absolute. In districts where a freehold or other system of building is universally accepted, builders will not build, and investors will not purchase, houses held on any different system ; and in such cases special powers have to be inserted in settlements, or even to be procured by private Act of Parliament. But still, in the majority of cases where land is settled, there is nothing like an equal choice between a long leasehold and a freehold system of building.

The effect of this interference with complete liberty is (as has been shown above) not to "rob" the builder, or subsequent owner of the ground-lease, for the benefit of the landowner; but to take from the tenant-for-life of the land a portion of the full rent of his land, and to accumulate for the benefit of the remainderman the portion so taken. But none the less is there a marked interference with liberty of contract which deprives the present system of the argument in its favour, which might otherwise be derived from the fact of its growth and existence.

For the future, I strongly advocate a change

in the law, under which every tenant-for-life should be empowered to grant the settled land in fee, subject to a rent-charge, and to give an option of purchase to a lessee. And these additional powers should also be extended to all ecclesiastical corporations, and (if they do not already possess it) to the Ecclesiastical Commissioners, with a direction in the last case to make fair use of the power. The widest powers have lately been given to limited owners by the Settled Land Act, 1882, and there can be no reason why this further power should not also be extended to them. They will have the same motive to avail themselves of the power that a fee-simple owner now has; namely, that they will be able to secure a higher present rent for their property than they could do if they let it on long lease. And this motive should be allowed to have its full operation in favour of a freehold system of house tenure.

With regard to the past, the more difficult question arises, whether the fact that the ground-lease system has arisen under conditions other than those of free contract, affords (when coupled with the other objections to the system) a sufficient reason for empowering the present holders of ground-leases to compulsorily acquire the freehold of their properties. After some hesitation, I should for my own part, be inclined to answer the question in the negative. But the majority of opinion may, perhaps, prove to be on the other side, and it is interesting, therefore, to inquire, upon *what* terms long-leaseholders ought to be empowered to acquire the freehold of their houses, assuming that on some terms or other this power ought to be given to them.

Now, first of all, it seems clear that no leaseholder should have the power of acquiring the freehold, unless his leasehold interest in the property is already of considerable value. For instance, no holder of an occupation-lease at a rack-rent should have this option. For he only took his lease for occupation purposes; gave *ex hypothesi* nothing for it; and will probably not be able to get anything for it, unless property has improved in the neighbourhood since the grant of the lease. Such a lease can hardly be highly beneficial, and may be actually onerous. And a person should have shown a deliberate intention of investing in the purchase of some very substantial interest in a house, before he is given the option of acquiring the entire interest in it. This consideration is fatal to Messrs. Broadhurst and Reid's proposal, to fix the number of years giving the right to purchase as low as 20 years. For 21 years is not an unusual occupation term for high-class property, and has, indeed, been recognised specially by the Parliamentary Franchise Acts.

Again, it may be doubted, whether the leaseholder should have power to purchase when, as sometimes happens, the leasehold interest is not as valuable as the freehold interest; as for instance, when the ground-rent is half or more than half the amount of the rack-rent.

Again, it seems clear, that leaseholders should not be given an indefinite time in which to purchase, after the passing of any Act on the subject. Such a power ought not to be kept longer than is absolutely necessary hanging over the heads of landowners; who after all are human, and do not enjoy arbitrary changes in the form of their property. A limit of 5 or 10 years for this purpose should be prescribed by any Act on the subject. And it would seem only right that (in imitation of the Copyhold Acts) the option should not be entirely on one side; but that the ground-landlord should be as able to insist on the ground-leaseholder purchasing the freehold, as the latter is to compel the ground-landlord to sell. For it must be remembered, that the reason put forward for the passing of an Act on the subject is, the desirability of terminating what is supposed to be a bad system.

And, lastly, any scheme for the compulsory expropriation of ground-landlords should contain provision to ensure that they are fully, even generously, compensated for the property they are deprived of. The present holders of ground-rents are not in the least to blame for any defects in the system of building leases. And if their investments are to be disturbed at the option of persons who never bargained for any such power, the greatest care should be taken that the fullest value be paid for the privilege. I was told some time since, by a builder in a large way of business, that the day after passing of a Leasehold Enfranchisement Act, he would serve notice on all his ground-landlords to purchase the fee. And he would no doubt be well advised in doing so. For, as pointed out in a previous chapter, the addition to the selling value of the houses, when converted into freehold, would be more than the addition to their strict actuarial value; while, on the other hand, the additional value imparted to a ground-rent, by the prospect of an ultimate reversion to the rack-rentals is very small indeed, and hardly, if at all, exceeds the actuarial value.

But if there is to be given to one class of persons a beneficial option of purchasing the property of another class, it can hardly be disputed that such a value should be set on the property as shall prevent any risk of loss to the class compelled to sell.

Now, in this respect, the Bill introduced by Mr. Broadhurst seems much inferior to that supported by Lord Randolph Churchill. For, while the former suggests that an *unwilling* vendor should be compelled to sell at the price at which a county court judge supposes that a *willing* vendor would sell; the latter proposes in important cases to employ the machinery of the Lands Clauses Acts, and in less important cases to make an addition to the price of

10 per cent. in respect of compulsory purchase.

That an *unwilling* vendor should be forced to sell at the same price as a *willing* vendor, and that too at any time selected by the purchaser, is a proposal so manifestly inequitable in its very statement as to need no further refutation. But it may well be that the provisions of the Lands Clauses Acts afford undue protection to vendors, and cast needlessly heavy burdens upon purchasers. And this is the view taken by Messrs. Broadhurst and Reid, who complain that under these provisions railway companies, and other great undertakings of the same class, have been " plundered " all over the country.

That railway and other companies have been compelled to pay, on the whole, exorbitant prices for their land can hardly be doubted by any one at all acquainted with the facts. But this seems to be due to the fact that the persons purchasing *are* great corporations, not merely to the enactments of the Lands Clauses Acts. In case of dispute, either party may insist on the price for the property taken being determined by a jury; and the kindness of juries to individuals when in dispute with corporations is unfortunately only too notorious. Now, though a jury may be summoned only in one case out of twenty, the price paid in the other nineteen cases is determined by an estimate of what a jury would probably give if recourse were had to them. It is quite true that if the jury ultimately fix on a price less than that already offered by the company, the claimant has to pay his own costs of the inquiry. But, in practice, companies find that the offer of a price is an invitation to a jury to slightly exceed that price; and such an offer, therefore, probably increases the price ultimately payable by the company, without relieving them of costs.

Now there is no reason to suppose that juries would exhibit any such sympathy as this with a landowner whose ground-rent was compulsorily taken by a leaseholder. In all probability their sympathies would be with the leaseholder, and when we add to this that the leaseholder would not have to pay compensation for "severance" to the same extent as a railway company, and remember that compensation for severance, though perfectly proper, is necessarily indefinite, and is often fixed unduly high as against a railway company, there seems good reason for thinking that in this case the machinery of the Lands Clauses Acts would not be productive of injustice to the purchaser. In two small points that machinery might, perhaps, be amended for this purpose. A fixed percentage of the value (say 10 per cent.) might be laid down as the proper compensation for compulsory purchase in all cases; while, in case the vendor refuses to accept a sum equal to, or higher than, that offered by the purchaser, the vendor might reasonably be made to pay the costs of the inquiry as to value on *both* sides. But, subject to these trifling alterations, the provisions of the Lands Clauses Acts seem reasonably applicable to the compulsory enfranchisement of leaseholds, should it be ultimately decided to take this novel step in legislation.

One concluding remark to that small class of persons who are always ready to assign the meanest motives for the treatment of a professional subject by a professional man. The effect of the passing of any effective measure of Leasehold Enfranchisement would be to increase the mass of conveyancing work done by professional men. This increase would be most considerable during the first few years after the passing of any Act, but would, to a lesser extent, probably be permanent, inasmuch as the length and difficulty of a freehold title are, as a rule, greater under the present law than those of a leasehold title.

CHAPTER VIII.

GROUND-RENTS, ON RE-LETTING, AND CHIEF RENTS.

IN the previous chapters of this book the case principally dealt with has been that where land is covered with buildings for the first time. Allusion has, however, from time to time been made to cases where the original building-leases fall in, and where building operations are recommenced on land which is already covered. It may therefore be desirable to devote a few paragraphs to the direct examination of these instances.

On the expiration of the original building-lease, the successor of the original landowner (whether claiming by descent, settlement, or purchase) becomes as fully and absolutely entitled to the land and buildings as his predecessor was to the land. He may, therefore, either receive the rack-rents of the houses, or he may, as is more usual, proceed to make a fresh building-lease for a longer or a shorter term than the original lease, according to circumstances. The bargain will be made, as a rule, with an outside builder or speculator, though sometimes the occupier or the owner of the expired ground-lease may undertake the contract, and the rent obtained by the landowner will be as pure a consequence of contract as in the case of previously undeveloped property. Inasmuch, however, as by the natural growth of population the land, which was 99 years ago on the outskirts of the town, is now relatively much more central, the value of the land, exclusive of the buildings on it, has probably increased very largely, and this circumstance will affect the contract made by the landowner in various ways.

If, for instance, the landowner determines to entirely rebuild, and to let the land for this purpose on a fresh 99 years' lease, he will be able to obtain a ground-rent much in excess of that which he previously received. For, to recur to the previous illustration of a house which was estimated by a builder to cost £2,000, and to produce a rack-rent of £140, it is obvious that, if the same class of house were built in a central position, instead of on the outskirts of the town, it would be worth a much higher rack-rent, say some £200 a year. But the builder, in order to obtain this price, has only, as before, to provide a beneficial annual rental of £125. It follows, then, that he can offer to the landowner, under these circumstances, a present ground-rent of £75 instead of £15.

But, instead of obtaining so large an increase in his ground-rent, the landowner may prefer to let his land for a shorter term, say 66 years, and to receive a smaller rent during the period. Taking the same instance as before, and estimating the value of a 66 years' lease at 15 years' purchase, this will work out as follows:—The builder, to secure his price of £2,000, will now have to provide a beneficial annual rental of £133 6s. 8d. He will, therefore, be able to offer for a 66 years' lease a rental of £66 13s. 4d. only. And here it may be incidentally remarked, that it is only where the value of the land bears a considerable proportion to the value of the buildings, that comparatively short building-leases will be possible. For, assuming that our land is once more on the outskirts of the town, and that a £2,000 house will only fetch £140 a year, our builder would only be able to offer a ground-rent of £6 13s. 4d. for a 66 years' lease instead of £15 for a 99 years' lease. And assuming (what is often the case) that such a house would only fetch £130 a year rack-rent, while the builder on a 99 years' lease would still be able to offer £5 a year ground-rent, the builder on a 66 years' lease would be unable to provide the necessary beneficial annual rental, unless he were not only rent free, but actually received an annual payment of £1 13s. 4d.

But, to recur again to the instance of the building-lease which has just expired, the landowner may find that entire rebuilding is unnecessary, and that repairs to the extent of £1,000 will be quite sufficient to make the house last, say for another 50 years. Suppose, then, that he decides to let the house again for the whole of this period, and that as a matter of fact a 50 years' lease is worth 14 years' purchase. The builder, who is to expend £1,000 (I suppose that, as before, this sum is comprehensive, and covers all cost, including ordinary profit), must now provide a beneficial annual rent of £1,000÷14, or £71 8s. 7d.; and he can, therefore, offer the landowner an annual rent for the 50 years' lease of £138 11s. 5d. It will be observed that this rent is not in any sense merely "ground"-rent, inasmuch as it includes a rent for buildings utilised by the builder.

Sometimes, in such a case as that last stated, the landowner will grant a lease for 21 years only; and, taking such a lease as worth 11 years' purchase, the figures will work out thus:—The builder has now to provide a beneficial annual rent of £1,000÷11, or £90 18s. 2d., and the rent he can offer to the landlord will, therefore, be £109 1s. 10d.

Sometimes, again, a landowner will have more substantial and expensive buildings erected, than would be the case if he looked only to obtaining the largest immediate ground-rent. But it is not necessary to work out the figures in this case, which will present no difficulties to any one who has grasped the previous instances. And, speaking generally, it may be asserted that, almost infinite as are the methods in which the landowner may realise the increased value of his property on the falling-in of the ground-leases, there is no one of these methods which enables him in any way to evade the ordinary laws of supply and demand. A perfectly well-understood and hardly-fought-out bargain is struck between the landowner and his new lessee—a bargain which is usually advantageous on both sides.

One additional feature of rebuilding, as distinguished from building, is, that in the former case there is much less of a speculative element, inasmuch as the rack-rentals of houses in an old district can be more certainly determined. And so, while such rapid fortunes can hardly be made by builders building over previously-covered ground, they are much less exposed to heavy loss. And here may, perhaps, be noticed a cry which is sometimes raised as to the hard terms of renewal *imposed* by landlords on the lessees or occupiers under an expired building-lease. Such lessees or occupiers have neither more nor less right to a renewal than any other person has to a new lease. But, inasmuch as they are on the spot at the termination of a lease, they often get the offer of a new lease on the terms which the landowner expects to obtain from some one or other. This offer they can always decline, if onerous ; while if it is, as often happens, beneficial, they have the first chance of accepting it. It follows, therefore, that such lessees or occupiers are in fact peculiarly favoured, as often obtaining a highly beneficial option, for which they never bargained.

In some parts of London, as for instance in the City, land has been let on many successive building-leases, and in such parts the rent of the ground often very largely exceeds the additional rent due to the buildings on it. It would serve no useful purpose to inquire in these pages, what the approximate relative values of the land and the buildings on it are in different parts of London. But any one at all interested in the subject may form some idea of the facts, by a study of the "sale advertisements" perpetually appearing in the daily papers. Thus, for instance, in the month of March last, there was an advertisement in the *Standard* of the sale of the unexpired leasehold interest in buildings near Holborn, from which it appeared that the land had been leased some forty or fifty years ago at a ground-rent equal to about half the present rack-rents.

In that district, therefore, land is now probably worth something more than the buildings on it. And rough information of this kind may be readily obtained in the same way with regard to every quarter of London. The only point necessary to be insisted on for the purpose of my argument is, that in every case the amount of the ground-rent obtained is the result of free contract, and of the ordinary laws of supply and demand.

It is obvious, that all that has been said in previous chapters with regard to the rating of ground-rents, and the enfranchisement of leaseholds, applies with as much force to ground-rents reserved on a second letting of property, as to original ground-rents on previously uncovered property. The lessees have covenanted to pay the rates; they have, as a matter of fact, deducted the *full* amount of the rates from the rents they have agreed to pay; they, or their tenants, are exclusively benefited by the expenditure of the greater part of the rates, and are primarily benefited by the expenditure of the remaining part; and any alteration in the present law would merely have the effect of transferring so much capital into their pockets from the pockets of the ground-landlords.

It may be interesting now to turn to another form of building contract, which has also been previously alluded to, namely, the grant of land in fee for building purposes subject to a rent-charge—a system analogous to that known in Scotland as feuing.

Since the statute of Quia Emptores, passed in the reign of Edward I., it has been impossible in England to reserve a rent on a grant in fee. And all the quit-rents and fee farm-rents, at present existing throughout England, must have been reserved (strange as it may seem) on a grant made before the passing of this statute. But the same effect is practically produced by the grant of lands in fee, subject to an over-riding rent-charge, and this process has been recently simplified by the Conveyancing and Law of Property Act, 1881, sec. 44. This system is extremely common in the North of England, where the rent-charges created under it are often and conveniently called chief-rents. The second chapter of this essay has already dealt, to some extent, with these chief-rents; for the purpose of instituting a comparison between the amount of chief-rent and ground-rent respectively obtainable for building purposes. But a more detailed examination of chief-rents may be interesting.

First, then, on the grant of land for building purposes in return for a chief-rent, the landowner's interest in the property is for ever limited to that chief-rent. He has no reversion in him, and no possibility of ever coming into possession of the rack-rents. He may have some interest in the enforcement of restrictive covenants, entered into for the benefit of adjoining property. But estate in the land he has none whatever. Provided his chief-rent is well secured, no improvement in the value of the land makes any addition to the value of his chief-rent, and no deterioration takes anything from it. In fact, he appears to be very much in the position of a man who has sold his land out-and-out, but with the difference that, instead of a lump sum down, he has commuted the price into a perpetual annuity.

The arrangement is a perfectly fair one, is not open to some of the objections of the ground-lease system, and is one which every tenant-for-life of settled land should have the option of entering into. But it has two main disadvantages. First, considerable complication of title is caused by the existence of all sorts of over-riding and over-lapping chief-rents. And secondly, the rent being fixed for convenience' sake in money, varies in actual value very greatly over long periods of time. Until quite recently, the variations have been much against landlords on the whole, as witness the insignificance of all existing quit-rents and fee farm-rents, when compared with the value of the land on which they are charged. But, if the present appreciation of gold continues, there may be a great change in the other direction, and then the disadvantage in question will be perhaps more keenly felt, certainly more keenly denounced.

Such being the nature of chief-rents, it would obviously be yet more inadmissible to rate them than to rate ground-rents. All the arguments previously put forward against the rating of ground-rents are equally fatal to any proposal to rate chief-rents. And beyond and above all these is the fact that no expenditure of rates whatever can benefit the owner of the chief-rent. He can never resume possession of the land, or extract one halfpenny more chief-rent, whatever the increased value of the land may be. And, therefore, there can be no reason whatever for subjecting him to rates. Indeed, the question would have appeared to me hardly worth arguing, had not an honourable member of Parliament complained in the recent debate on the 16th March last, that there was a member of the House of Commons "who drew £50,000 in feu duties from the City of Glasgow, and did not contribute a penny to the rates." * The magnitude of the sum in question probably obscured the honourable member's reasoning faculties.

In some districts, again, the custom is to let on building lease for terms of 999 years, or even longer. Such leases need not detain us here. They lie somewhere between a ninety-nine years' lease and a grant in fee. Legally they are analogous to the former. Practically they approximate much more nearly to the latter, inasmuch as a reversion, to fall into possession eight or nine hundred years hence, is absolutely worthless, whatever the value of the property.

---

* *Times* Report, March 17th.

As the subject of rating has again been touched on, a few words may be added as to the proposal to rate on its capital value land rapidly increasing in value by reason of its proximity to a great town. The object of course is to prevent landowners keeping their land back from the building market with a view to subsequently obtaining a higher rent or price. Nor can there be said to be anything illegitimate, unfair, or confiscatory about the proposal, if the change be gradually and temperately made.

At the same time there appear to be serious objections to the proposal. There would be much difficulty in assessing the capital value of such land, there would be hardship in enforcing payment of a rate sometimes perhaps actually exceeding the rents derived from the land, and there are well-known economical objections to any tax on savings. But the answer that should be given to the proposal seems to me mainly to depend upon the answer to a previous question, which is this: Is land on the whole unduly held back from the building market, or is the present tendency rather to push it into that market before the proper time? Different answers will be probably given to this question, according to the neighbourhood with which the respondent is best acquainted. But from those who are at all acquainted with land on the outskirts of London, who have seen notices of land to let for building purposes budding forth in suitable and unsuitable spots alike, and who have marked the advertisements of building estates in the London papers, there would probably be an almost unanimous testimony that landowners are if anything over-eager to turn their properties into building estates. And if this be so it would be obviously unwise to do anything to increase the rush.

It must be remembered that, though landowners are not rated on increased value while it is accruing, they are rated on it to the full directly they come to enjoy the benefit of the increased income; paying, as I have endeavoured to show, the rates on the full rack-rentals of the houses built on their properties.

CHAPTER IX.

THE DETERMINATION OF RACK-RENT AND MONOPOLY.

IT is sometimes stated, that the system of ground-leases largely increases occupation or rack-rents; and the assertion, if substantial, would be a very serious impeachment of the system. The high rack-rents in London are often quoted in support of the assertion; but the fact is forgotten that in many continental capitals, where the ground-lease system is unknown, and notably in Paris, occupation rents are as high as, or higher than, those in London. It may be interesting, therefore, to consider rather more fully than was done in the second chapter, what are the causes which determine the amount of rent which an occupier contracts to pay to his landlord.

Now in this investigation I shall assume, that the Ricardian theory of rent is established. The theory is enforced by John Stuart Mill, is fully recognised even by Henry George, and has, in its main features, been accepted as unquestionable by one of the latest writers on the subject, Mr. Henry Sidgwick.* It has, moreover, a force and cogency of its own, which render it irresistible, when once it is fully understood.

The theory is generally stated with regard to agricultural land, that being the kind of land of the greatest importance to the political economist. It is assumed (though the truth of the assumption is not vital to the theory) that there is in any one stage of society, land just on the margin of cultivation, that is land which can just be cultivated so as to yield average interest and profit on the capital employed, if no rent is paid for it. It is then asserted, that the rent paid for any superior land is the measure of the superiority for production, which this land possesses over the land just on the margin of cultivation. And the consequence follows, that as the necessities of increasing population compel resort to the cultivation of soil inferior to the least productive soil previously cultivated, the rents of all lands

---

* See " Principles of Political Economy," Chapter VII.

previously cultivated must rise, inasmuch as their superiority is increased, when tested with reference to a lowered standard.

Now, precisely the same line of reasoning is applicable to the occupation-rents of houses. There are, of course, many sites in the kingdom where it would not pay to build a house rent-free. That is, an occupation-rent could not be obtained for the house sufficient to afford ordinary interest on the sum expended in its construction, or in other words the occupation-rent would be so low, that a purchaser buying on this rent would give a price less than the sum that had been expended in the construction of the buildings. But in the infinite and continuous gradations of suitability in sites for the erection of houses, there are many sites to be found, where it would just pay, and no more than pay, to erect a house rent-free. That is, the occupation-rent which would there be obtained for a house, would be just sufficient, and no more than sufficient, to yield an ordinary profit on the cost of construction, or in other words, to induce a purchaser to purchase at the actual cost of construction.

Such land as has just been mentioned may

be said to lie on the building limit. And the Ricardian theory may be said to be more obviously true with regard to houses, than with regard to agricultural land. For while it is difficult to point out agricultural land actually let without rent, it is easy enough to point out houses, or even whole neighbourhoods of houses, which from various causes are now let at a rent only sufficient, or even less than sufficient, to yield ordinary profit on their mere cost of construction.

Now, assuming that a house just on the building limit is let at a rack-rent of £50, the rack-rent of a similar house in a more favourite district will exceed this sum of £50 by an amount which measures the superiority for residential or business purposes, in the eye of an occupier, of the second position over the first. Now, as population increases, and the less and less favoured sites are built over, the difference for residential purposes between the sites on the building limit and the picked sites, which have long since been built over, becomes more and more marked. And as the rent for the house on the picked site exceeds that for the house on the building margin in proportion to this superiority, while there is no reason for supposing that the rent of the house on the building limit (that is the rent for the mere buildings) will at all decrease, the consequence is, that the rents for houses on the picked sites must, on the whole, tend continually to increase.

The consequence, therefore, of the mere increase of town population, and of the continually increasing invasion of country by town, is to raise the occupation-rents of all houses previously existing, so far of course as an equilibrium is maintained between houses and occupiers. And stated as an equation, the occupation-rent of such houses = rent for buildings + superiority of residential advantages over houses on the building limit. If, then, the 2nd term on the right-hand side of the equation is continually increasing, while the 1st term is on the average about stationary, the only term on the left-hand side of the equation must necessarily also increase. Now the cost of buildings, and the rent for buildings alone, must under any given system of building, and apart from wide fluctuations in wages and prices, be fairly constant. The result of the equation may therefore be stated in at least two ways. First, as a town increases, and less and less suitable land is built over, occupation-rents in the town will increase. Or, secondly, as occupation-rents increase in a town, less and less suitable land in its suburbs will be built over.

One further point in this equation should be noticed, and that is, that not merely the increase, but the *whole* increase in occupation-rents, is due to the resort to less and less suitable land. For systems of building do *not* readily change, and under any given system, the cost and rent of buildings are constant. Any fluctuation in occupation-rents must therefore be due simply and solely to some fluctuation in the nature of the land which from time to time forms the building limit. In other words, the growth of house-rent is due entirely to the increase of towns.

One other point, however, has yet to be inquired into. It has been shown that the rack-rents of houses are composed of two items, one of which is the rent of the actual buildings. Now, it has been asserted, and seems undoubtedly true, that *under any given system* this portion of the rent must remain about constant. May it not be, however, that one system of building may necessitate a higher rent for buildings than another system?

This higher rent might be due to either of two causes, first, an increased cost of construction, or, secondly, an increased rate of interest habitually demanded by the investor in buildings. Now, there seems no reason for supposing that the ground-lease system adds anything to the cost of construction of houses. Indeed, it probably effects to some extent a saving in legal charges, though any such saving must necessarily be very slight, probably, indeed, inappreciable, in relation to the whole cost of a house. But, on the other hand, it does seem to be the fact, that the ground-lease system tends to place a higher rent on buildings, than does the freehold system. For under the former system, an investor gives a smaller number of years' purchase for his house, than under the latter. Or, in other words, he expects to make a higher rate of interest, and that independently of any sinking fund.

Let us recur to the illustration, given in the

second chapter, of a house, the cost of production of which is £2,000. If the builder only obtains and sells a leasehold interest in this house he can only procure sixteen years' purchase for his interest, and he is bound, therefore, to provide a purchaser with a beneficial annual value of £125. In other words, the rent for the buildings is £125 annually. If, on the other hand, the builder can sell a freehold interest in the house, he can procure seventeen years' purchase for this interest, and he need only provide a beneficial annual value of £117 12s. 11d. That is, the rent for the buildings is now only £117 12s. 11d. The difference of £7 7s. 1d. between the two rents appears to me attributable to the leasehold system.*

But, it may be said that, in the case referred to, the *occupier* offers £140 in either case to the builder or ground lessee; that the occupier is (as previously stated) not concerned with, or affected by, any bargain between his immediate landlord and any superior landlord; that the £7 7s. 1d. is the exact reduction of rent to

* See Note (8).

which the landowner has to submit; and that he is the sole sufferer, not the occupier.

The objection is tenable only when the case is considered of a house built during the continuance of an already existing system. If the rent for such a house as has been instanced *is* £140, then it is quite true that the landowner, and the landowner alone, will lose by granting a long lease only instead of the fee. But, when the comparison is one between systems, the case is altered. Under a general freehold system, the rent for the house in question would, as I believe, be not £140 but £132 12s. 11d., and this for the following reason. Under a general freehold system a house, built as this is for £2,000, could just be profitably erected and let *on the building limit* for £117 12s. 11d.; while under the leasehold system the necessary rent would be £125. Now if, under a leasehold system of house tenure, £15 a year just measures in the eye of the occupier the superiority of a house in a certain neighbourhood over a similar house on the building limit, there is no reason for thinking that this superiority between situations will either increase or decrease in consequence of a change in the building system. If, therefore, under a freehold system an occupier can obtain a house on the building limit for £117 12s. 11d. instead of £125, he will only offer for a house in a neighbourhood superior to the extent of £15 per annum, a rent of £132 12s. 11d. instead of £140. And this reasoning will be further confirmed by an attentive study of the equation determining the amount of occupation-rent which has been stated above.

It appears, therefore, that to some extent, a general system of ground-leases *does* increase the rent to the occupier. But the extent is probably slight; affects only that part of the rent of a house which represents rent on buildings, and has nothing to do with the general *growth* of rents in towns.

It may now be interesting to touch on the question of the real or supposed monopoly of land, as affecting house-rents. And in the first place, it is necessary to point out that the word monopoly is often improperly used in this connection. Land is sometimes said to be a monopoly because it is limited in extent. But however limited it may be, so far as it is in the hands of a sufficient number of persons to prevent anything like a ring, and to ensure free competition of sellers in the market, it is not a monopoly in the economic sense. And the price which it will fetch, either on purchase or hire, will be determined, not by any law of monopoly, but by the ordinary laws of supply and demand.

Now the land about London, at any rate, is in an immense number of hands, and extreme competition exists between the different owners. So that here, at least, there is no *prima facie* occasion to inquire into the effects of monopoly.

It is said, however, that certain quarters or districts of the town, such, for instance, as the Bloomsbury district, are in individual hands; that large classes of professional men and others are compelled by the necessities of their business to reside in the Bloomsbury district, and that, consequently, rents in such a district rise to exorbitant price, to the advantage of the ground landlord.

If there is such a rise in rents in the Bloomsbury district, the whole increase will, no doubt, *ultimately* belong to the ground landlord, in this case, the Duke of Bedford; though *immediately* the persons to benefit will be the present ground lessees. But in order that such a phenomenon may occur, it is necessary that there should be a *professional* demand for houses in this quarter exceeding or nearly equalling the number of houses existing there. For a landlord who studies his own interest must always keep all, or nearly all, his houses occupied. And unless there is a professional demand for the vast majority of his houses, he must let a considerable proportion to residents who reside there merely for ordinary residential reasons. But if this is so, the rents in all cases must be on an ordinary residential level, since distinctions cannot be drawn between those tenants who are compelled to reside in the district and those who have merely the ordinary residential reasons for preferring it. And with regard to the Bloomsbury district, there is no reason to suppose that the larger proportion of the houses are occupied by persons who are practically *bound* to live there.

Near London, then, there is no reason to suppose that monopoly practically influences the rents of houses. But it is no doubt the case that the ground of some few of our provincial towns is either monopolised in one hand, or divided between so small a number of proprietors that an economic monopoly may be formed by union among them. In such a case the rents of houses may be raised to occupiers, either by limiting the number of houses allowed to be built, or by granting such short building-leases that a large rent has to be exacted by the lessee in proportion to the cost of construction, or in both of these ways. And in this way serious mischief may theoretically, and is, perhaps, sometimes practically, done to the development and prosperity of the town in question.

It must, however, be remembered that landowners cannot act in this manner without injuring their own interest. For though one town may be monopolised, there are other towns in full competition with it in other parts of the country. Any such attempt at monopoly, as has been described, will undoubtedly drive tenants away to other parts of the kingdom, to the great ultimate loss of the monopolists. And, therefore, no landowner acting in obedience to "enlightened self-interest" would press, or join in pressing, any such power of monopoly to any harsh extent.

Still, it would be poor consolation to any town, whose prosperity should be imperilled by the ill-advised exaction of a monopolist, that the monopolist was himself the chief loser by his folly. And, if any municipal corporation could prove to the satisfaction of Parliament that land in and about their district was in fact monopolised, and that the exactions of the monopolist or monopolists seriously affected the prosperity and development of their town, a case would be, in my view, established for compulsory interference.

In any such case the procedure should be by private bill legislation. The preamble of the bill should state the monopoly and the consequent injury to the prosperity of the town, and would have to be strictly proved. The enacting part would provide for the letting of land for building purposes by some impartial person or tribunal at a fair price, having regard to the rents obtained in similar districts where no monopoly existed.

But the cases in which such application would have to be made would be very few, if, indeed, there were any.

CHAPTER X.

GENERAL REMARKS AND CONCLUSION.

IN the preceding chapters an attempt has been made to show that the case against 99 years' building-leases has been grossly overstated; that the creation of a freehold system of tenure would affect the position of occupiers but very slightly for the better, and in some respects actually for the worse; and that the holder of ground-rents is not a public robber. It may now be of service to inquire, Who are the present holders of ground-rents; that is, Who are the persons whose interests would be mainly affected by the proposed changes in legislation?

Primarily, of course, ground-rents were the property of the landowners—sometimes small and sometimes great—who let their lands for building purposes. Now, just at the present moment, even the smallest landowner is viewed with the eye of suspicion, while great landowners are generally understood to be outside

K

the pale of humanity. So that, if they alone were concerned, there might be the gravest danger of hasty and oppressive legislation.

But although on many of the large residential estates in and about London, the ground-rents are still held in one hand, in many other districts ground-rents are almost indefinitely subdivided amongst purchasers and sub-purchasers from the original owners. These purchases have, in a very large number of cases, been made at public auctions, where the holders of the ground-leases subject to the ground-rents have had an opportunity (which they have not taken) of purchasing these ground-rents, and thus acquiring the fee simple of their houses. The purchasers, again, are of every grade of society, and do not in any marked degree consist of those who are sometimes styled the "landowning classes." They are often not landowners at all, except in respect of the particular ground-rents they have purchased.

But, further, these investors are of a class who are content with a small return on their capital, so long as they can obtain a fixed income and perfect security. They are the same class who invest in Consols, in Corporation Stocks, in the Debenture and Preference Stock of first-class railways, and in other high-class securities of the same description. Trustees, retired professional men, spinsters, Fire and Life Assurance Companies of all kinds, and, in fact, all persons and corporations who require an income well-secured, fixed, and free from trouble and anxiety, form the bulk of the investors in ground-rents.

Now, nothing is more marked in our present highly-developed state of society than the tendency to differentiate investments into the more and the less speculative. This is due partly to the fact that almost every trader can employ in his business a larger amount of capital than he actually possesses, and is therefore inclined to use borrowed money, which is better secured, but earns less interest, than his own capital. Instances of this may be found in the shipowner with mortgages on his ships, the manufacturer with mortgages on his mills, or the builder with mortgages on his building agreements and on his houses. Or, to take another example, a tradesman in Liverpool can afford to give £2000 for a freehold shop subject to a chief-rent worth £2000, when it would be excessively awkward for him to provide a sum of £4000 for the purchase of a shop subject to no chief-rent at all. Indeed, in the latter case he would probably have to borrow a sum of £2000 on mortgage of the shop, and would thus afford but another illustration of the rule in question.

But beyond the distinction between the trader and his mortgagee (who for some purposes resemble the active and the sleeping partners in a firm) is the further division between the secured and the unsecured portions of investments pure and simple. The most familiar examples of the kind are the preference* and ordinary stocks of railways, canals, docks, gas and water-works, and other great undertakings of the kind. In all these cases the total profits of the undertakings are first applied in paying small fixed dividends on the preference stocks, and the balance is then devoted to paying dividends (generally larger, but more fluctuating) on the ordinary stocks. But to many

---

* The holders of debenture stocks are rather in the position of mortgagees, and come under the head first mentioned.

investors the uncertainty even of these ordinary stocks is not sufficient, while some addition to the security of these stocks is palatable to other investors. And so in several railway companies the ordinary stock is actually subdivided into preferred and deferred stock, the deferred stock taking nothing till a considerable dividend has been paid on the preferred stock.

In this last instance, the differentiation of interests may, perhaps, have been carried too far; but it well illustrates the tendency of investors to divide themselves into two classes, the one seeking high profits, the other perfect security.

Each class of investors is entitled to the consideration of Government; but if a distinction is to be made, it should be in favour of the second class. They are the more steady, the more careful, and the more provident of two classes; and, indeed, constitute the "salt" of the investing classes. And I still cling to the old-fashioned notion, that it is the duty of Government to encourage and not to discourage steadiness, providence, and self-restraint.

Now, taking rates at an average of 4s. or 5s. in the £, the effect of rating ground-rents would be to take from this class of investors from 20 to 25 per cent. of their incomes, while the capital value of their property would probably be yet more seriously injured. A more cruel and wanton interference with a most deserving class of persons it would be difficult to imagine. An instance may be mentioned which has recently come to my knowledge, and which is only typical of thousands of others. A professional man, with several unmarried daughters, has provided for them, by investing the whole of the savings of a life's hard work in the purchase of ground-rents. The passing of a measure for the rating of ground-rents will deprive these ladies of a fifth, a quarter, or an even more considerable proportion of their incomes.

The wrong done will, in fact, be the more cruel the smaller the investor. The wealthy nobleman, with £50,000 a year from ground-rents, can be mulcted of £12,500 a year, and yet be reasonably well off, though this would not, of course, justify the robbery. But the spinster, or widow, with an income of £100 a year from ground-rents cannot submit to a deprivation of one-fourth of her income without the extremest hardship.

Again, with regard to the enfranchisement of leaseholds, if a certain and very considerable public benefit would accrue from the passing of the measure, it is right and just that the benefit of the public should prevail over other considerations. But if the good to be done by such a measure is at best uncertain, and at most inconsiderable, the convenience of investors is entitled to the fullest consideration, as itself forming one item of public advantage. In any case, if ground-lessees are to have the option given to them of purchasing the ground-rents to which their leases are subject, it must be under conditions which will fully protect those whose properties are compulsorily taken.

One last illustration may be given, which is almost a *reductio ad absurdum* of the position taken by one at least of the more prominent of the advocates of leasehold enfranchisement. Mr. Broadhurst is reported to have complained, at a recent meeting of the Leasehold Enfranchisement Society, that while the occupation value of his house had lately decreased some 10 or 20 per cent., the ground-rent on it *remained fixed*. The complaint may be advantageously compared with the suggestion of a recent correspondent of the *Pall Mall Gazette*, to the effect that mortgages should abate in proportion to any reduction in the value of the properties on which they are secured.

Destructive criticism is not by itself a very satisfying form of mental diet, and a writer is generally expected to conclude with construction of one kind or another. In the previous pages some indications have from time to time been given of the changes in the law which appear to me desirable; but it may be well to deal here, shortly and directly, with the subject. It need hardly be said that the following views, which necessarily trench on portions of far wider subjects than those mainly treated of in these pages, are put forward with the utmost hesitation and diffidence.

It is clear that the law may properly forbid contracts obviously detrimental to the well-being of society; and may as legitimately fix a minimum of sanitary requirement, as of education. Indeed, both these principles have frequently been recognised in our statute-book. But, further, the law should rather aim at the diffusion of property amongst many, than at its concentration in the hands of a few; should discourage any system hampering freedom of contract; and should render the transfer of land as simple and expeditious as possible. The practical proposals which appear best calculated to carry out these principles and effect these objects are the following, none of which have, of course, any claim to originality :—

1. The prohibition of leases for uncertain periods, such as leases for lives.

2. The strict enforcement of a certain minimum of sanitary requirements in dwelling houses.

3. The abolition of the law of primogeniture.

4. The repeal of the statute *De Donis* (" law of entail.")*

5. The conferring on the tenant-for-life, under a settlement, on ecclesiastical and collegiate corporations, and on the Ecclesiastical Commissioners, of powers to grant in fee subject to a rent charge, or to give an option of purchase to their lessees.

6. The discharge of purchasers from any obligation to inquire into the trusts of land; settled land to be absolutely vested in trustees,

---

* See Note (5).

who may deal with it in any way as far as regards the safety of purchasers.

7. In cases of gross abuse of land monopoly, the bestowal on municipal corporations of a right to appeal to Parliament, and the nomination by Parliament of a body or person empowered to let or sell the land at fair prices, having regard to those obtained in similar districts.

Most of these proposals carry their object on the face of them. But, with regard to No. 2, it may be remarked that its tendency will be very slightly to increase the rents of the poorer classes, though with more than counterbalancing advantage to them. Again, Nos. 5 and 6 are not really in conflict, as might appear at first sight. For the tenant-for-life would call on the trustees to exercise towards a lessee or purchaser the powers conferred on him. The result of the other proposals should be to ensure, with regard to land, the unhampered operation of the ordinary laws of supply and demand. And, in the resulting battle of the various building systems, there can be but little doubt that the fittest will survive.

NOTES.

NOTES.

1.—For instance, a landowner has, we will suppose, building land just worth £100,000. If he lets the whole land to builders, and obtains well-secured ground-rents, his resulting income will be some £4,000 a year. If, on the other hand, he sells off the greater part of the land, and with the proceeds of sale just covers the residue with houses, he will now have £100,000 in freehold house property, and his income will be from £5,500 to £6,000 a year. The justification of these figures will be found in the second chapter, and the explanation of the difference between them in the third and tenth chapters.

2.—Practical men will say that the *whole* prospective increase or decrease does not, as a matter of fact, accrue to or fall on the landowner. But practical men are apt to consider relatively small periods of time, and to instance cases in which builders are already in touch with a landowner. No doubt, important causes do not produce their *full* results for some time; and where land has once been let to a builder on certain terms, the strong tendency is to let further land to him on *about* the same terms. But, ultimately, it seems to me undeniable that the landowner is the only person to gain or lose.

It may be noted that where a neighbourhood is deteriorating, the immediate ground-rent to the landowner is sometimes kept up by covering ground very thickly with an inferior class of property. But this is clearly no exception to the rule.

3.—In comparing the ground-lease system with a freehold system, I have throughout considered that form of the latter system under which a rent-charge or chief-rent is fixed, not that form which consists of a sale for a capital sum.

It is more convenient to compare two annual payments than to compare an annual payment with a capital sum. It may be added that in describing or comparing the building-lease system, I have, in general, had in view the 99 years' system.

4.—In the instance worked out, I have assumed the price of a freehold house as being one year's purchase more than that of a leasehold house. This may probably be an underestimate. But were freeholds to become as numerous as leaseholds, the difference in price might probably become much less marked than is the case at present.

5.—By the statute De Donis, passed in the reign of Edward I., all alienations of estates tail were forbidden. But this law was soon evaded in practice, and the practice was legislatively recognised and amended by the Fines and Recoveries Act, passed in the year 1833. As the law now stands, a tenant-in-tail in possession can, by the execution and enrolment of a disentailing deed, acquire the absolute fee-simple of the entailed land. But a tenant-in-tail in remainder, which is the position of the "heir apparent" to an estate during his father's life-time, cannot, without his father's consent (or that of some other protector of the settlement), acquire the fee-simple in remainder of the land;

but can, at most, only obtain a much more unmarketable estate, called a base fee.

The consequence of this highly artificial state of the law is that the heir apparent is, to some extent, at the mercy of his father, who, as the condition of an allowance during the bachelorhood of his son, and a provision for his wife and children in case of marriage, can insist upon a strict resettlement of the estate.

6.—It will again be said that, *practically*, rates do not fall to their full extent on ground-rents. Much of what is said in Note 2 might be repeated here. But there is this further consideration, that a large part of the expenditure of the rates is beneficial to occupiers, and so increases rent. This really means that this part of the rates is not borne in the sense of being a burden on any one, as he who pays for it gains by it. But, so far as the rates are actually borne by any one, it seems to me that the *ultimate* sufferer is the landowner.

7.—One more instance may be given of the sort of animus which disfigures Messrs. Broadhurst and Reid's book. On page 18 they state that in leases for lives the life of the Prince of Wales used often to be chosen, " probably on the ground that his Royal Highness was always likely to be well looked after in case of illness." The suggested contrast between the well-cared-for Prince and the down-trodden and neglected peasant is unmistakeable.

Now, as a matter of fact, princes are exposed to special temptations and special dangers, and are not a particularly long-lived class. The life of the Prince of Wales was, of course, selected merely because his death would be notorious, and so no dispute of fact could arise on the subject.

8.—The greater part of this extra rent of £7 7s. 1d. represents what may be called the sentimental objection of investors to a terminable investment, and only a small part represents the necessary sinking fund. That part which represents sentiment is clearly an addition due to the leasehold system; and the same appears also to be the case with the sinking fund itself. For, while on a freehold system the "building limit" is land on which no chief-rent can be paid, the "building limit" goes no lower under the leasehold system. A landowner would never offer to an intending lessee, in expectation of the reversion to the buildings to be erected, any annual payment equivalent to the sinking fund for those buildings. Or, to put the matter more practically, if £1 is the lowest chief-rent any landowner will accept for a house, there is no reason to think he will take a lower sum as ground-rent in consideration of his ultimate reversion.

I am here, of course, as in most places, speaking of a 99 years' lease. Any income expected by the owner of a 999 years' lease in excess of the income from a freehold would be purely "sentimental."

It should be noted, too, that the statement in Chap. IV., as to the occupier being unaffected by any bargain between his landlord and any superior landlord, is quite true *under an existing system*. When the possibility of an entire change of system is considered, the statement requires the slight modification pointed out in Chap. IX. But the trifling increase of rent caused by the leasehold system cannot, of course, be properly styled "robbery." In any case, it goes, in the main, to the owner of the ground-lease.

www.ingramcontent.com/pod-product-compliance
Lightning Source LLC
Chambersburg PA
CBHW030256170426
43202CB00009B/762